THE LOST RV CAMPING BIBLE

BIBLE

[15 IN 1]

Embark on the Ultimate Road Trip with 200+ Campgrounds and Must-Visit Attractions Across the US to Create Lasting Memories through Unforgettable Adventures

Jake Harrison

Text Copyright © [Jake Harrison]

Legal & Disclaimer

The information contained in this book and its contents is not designed to replace or take the place of any form of medical or professional advice; and is not meant to replace the need for independent medical, financial, legal or other professional advice or services, as may be required. The content and information in this book have been provided for educational and entertainment purposes only.

The content and information contained in this book has been compiled from sources deemed reliable, and it is accurate to the best of the Author's knowledge, information and belief. However, the Author cannot guarantee its accuracy and validity and cannot be held liable for any errors and/or omissions. Further, changes are periodically made to this book as and when needed. Where appropriate and/or necessary, you must consult a professional (including but not limited to your doctor, attorney, financial advisor or such other professional advisor) before using any of the suggested remedies, techniques, or information in this book.

Upon using the contents and information contained in this book, you agree to hold harmless the Author from and against any damages, costs, and expenses, including any legal fees potentially resulting from the application of any of the information provided by this book. This disclaimer applies to any loss, damages or injury caused by the use and application, whether directly or indirectly, of any advice or information presented, whether for breach of contract, tort, negligence, personal injury, criminal intent, or under any other cause of action.

You agree to accept all risks of using the information presented inside this book.

You agree that by continuing to read this book, where appropriate and/or necessary, you shall consult a professional (including but not limited to your doctor, attorney, or financial advisor or such other advisor as needed) before using any of the suggested remedies, techniques, or information in this book.

Table of Contents

Introduction **5**

History and Evolution 5

Types of RVs 7

Book 1: Choosing the Right RV **9**

Buying vs. Renting 9

RV Features 11

Book 2: Planning Your RV Adventure **14**

Route Planning 14

Itinerary Flexibility 16

Book 3: RV Maintenance and Safety **19**

Pre-Trip Checks 19

Basic Maintenance 21

Book 4: Navigating RV Parks and Campgrounds **26**

Choosing Campgrounds 26

Etiquette 29

Book 5: Living Comfortably in Your RV **33**

Packing Essentials 33

Organization Tips 37

Book 6: Budgeting for RV Travel **40**

Cost Breakdown 40

Money-Saving Tips 42

Book 7: Traveling with Family **45**

Family-Friendly Activities 45

Education on the Road 47

Book 8: Working and RVing **50**

Remote Work.. 50

Connectivity Solutions 53

Book 9: Exploring National Parks and Landmarks **56**

Highlighting Key Destinations...56

Guided Tours...64

Book 10: Culinary Adventures on the Road **69**

RV Cooking Tips 69

Local Cuisine...71

Book 11: Connecting with the RV Community **73**

Socializing on the Road...73

RV Clubs and Gatherings...74

Book 12: Environmental Responsibility.. **77**

Leave No Trace Principles 77

Eco-Friendly RV Practices 78

Book 13: Overcoming Challenges **80**

Common Challenges 80

Emergency Preparedness...81

Book 14: Exploring Top America's Campgrounds **84**

Special Features of Selected Campgrounds 86

Book 15: Reflecting on the Journey.. **98**

Journaling and Documentation 98

Memorable Moments 99

Conclusion **101**

Introduction

History and Evolution

(Photo of RDNE Stock project www.pexels.com)

Embarking on a journey across the vast and diverse landscapes of the United States in a Recreational Vehicle (RV) is more than a mode of travel; it's a lifestyle embraced by a multitude of enthusiasts. This unique way of exploring the country has gained immense popularity, attracting individuals with a shared passion for adventure, nature, and the freedom to traverse the open road. Understanding the diverse profiles and motivations of those who love RV travel requires delving into the rich history and evolution of RVs, a journey that spans decades and has significantly shaped American travel culture.

History and Evolution:

The roots of RV travel can be traced back to the early 20th century, a period marked by the rise of automobile culture and a newfound sense of wanderlust. The first recognizable RVs emerged as modified automobiles, with adventurous souls converting their vehicles into mobile homes for extended journeys. However, it wasn't until the 1930s that RVs, in a more recognizable form, began to gain traction.

During the Great Depression, as economic hardships prevailed, Americans sought affordable and flexible ways to travel. This era witnessed the birth of iconic trailers and motorhomes, with companies like Airstream pioneering sleek and aerodynamic designs. The 1950s brought about a surge in RV popularity, aligning with the post-war economic boom and the desire for leisurely exploration.

The 1960s and 1970s witnessed further innovation, with the introduction of amenities that transformed RVs into true homes on wheels. Features such as kitchens, bathrooms, and sleeping quarters became standard, catering to a growing demographic of families and retirees seeking comfort on their journeys. As the oil crisis of the 1970s impacted travel habits, smaller, more fuel-efficient RVs gained favor.

The 21st century ushered in a new era for RVs, marked by technological advancements, eco-conscious designs, and an increasing appeal to a diverse range of travelers. The industry saw the integration of solar power, smart home technologies, and sustainable materials. This evolution not only addressed environmental concerns but also catered to the preferences of tech-savvy nomads seeking connectivity on the road.

Today, RVs come in various shapes and sizes, from compact camper vans to luxurious motorhomes, accommodating the preferences and needs of a broad spectrum of travelers. The history and evolution of RVs not only reflect the changes in transportation and manufacturing but also mirror the evolving desires of a society that cherishes the freedom to roam and explore.

As RVs continued to evolve, their significance in American travel culture became deeply ingrained. The appeal of RV travel lies not just in the convenience and comfort they offer but in the freedom they afford individuals to tailor their journeys according to personal preferences. The RV, once a symbol of practicality during challenging economic times, transformed into an emblem of adventure and exploration.

Throughout the years, RV travel became synonymous with the spirit of the open road, embodying the American ethos of manifest destiny and the pursuit of new horizons. The ability to traverse the diverse landscapes of the USA, from the rugged mountains to the sun-kissed deserts, became a rite of passage for those seeking a genuine connection with the natural beauty that the country has to offer.

Moreover, RVs fostered a sense of community among travelers. RV parks and campgrounds emerged as hubs of social interaction, where individuals from different walks of life converged to share stories, tips, and the camaraderie born from a shared love of the road. These communal spaces added a social dimension to RV travel, creating a unique subculture that celebrates the freedom to roam while forming lasting connections.

The evolution of RVs also responded to changing societal trends. The increasing number of retirees adopting RV living as a full-time lifestyle, the rise of digital nomads utilizing modern amenities for remote work, and the growing awareness of eco-conscious practices are all testament to the adaptability and relevance of RVs in contemporary American culture.

The history and evolution of RVs in the USA narrate a captivating story of innovation, adaptation, and the enduring spirit of exploration. From humble beginnings as makeshift mobile homes to the sophisticated and diverse range of options available today, RVs continue to be a symbol of freedom, adventure, and the unyielding desire to hit the open road, creating a legacy deeply woven into the fabric of American travel culture.

Types of RVs

Recreational Vehicles (RVs) come in a diverse array of types, each designed to cater to different preferences, lifestyles, and travel needs. From spacious motorhomes to compact camper vans, the RV market offers a wide range of options, allowing adventurers to find the perfect mobile abode for their journeys.

1. Motorhomes:

Motorhomes, also known as RVs or motor coaches, are self-contained homes on wheels. They integrate living quarters with the vehicle chassis, providing a seamless and comfortable travel experience. Motorhomes are further classified into three main types:

Class A: These are the largest and most luxurious motorhomes, often resembling buses. They offer spacious interiors with amenities such as full kitchens, bathrooms, and entertainment systems. Class A motorhomes are ideal for long-term travelers or those seeking a home-like experience on the road.

Class B: Also known as camper vans, Class B motorhomes are more compact and versatile. They are built on van chassis, making them easier to maneuver and park. Despite their smaller size, Class B motorhomes can still include essential amenities, making them a popular choice for solo travelers and couples.

Class C: Combining features of both Class A and Class B, Class C motorhomes are characterized by a distinctive over-cab section. This space often houses an additional sleeping area, making them suitable for families. Class C motorhomes strike a balance between size and amenities, offering a comfortable travel experience.

2. Travel Trailers:

Travel trailers are towable RVs that attach to a separate vehicle, providing flexibility for travelers who prefer not to drive a large motorhome. These trailers come in various sizes and styles, accommodating different preferences:

Conventional Travel Trailers: These trailers come in a wide range of sizes and floor plans, offering amenities such as kitchens, bathrooms, and sleeping quarters. They are towed by trucks or SUVs, making them a popular choice for families and those who appreciate the ability to unhitch and explore in a separate vehicle.

Fifth-Wheel Trailers: Similar to conventional travel trailers, fifth-wheel trailers attach to the bed of a pickup truck using a specialized hitch. The unique design allows for increased stability and often includes spacious living areas and multiple slide-outs, providing additional interior space when parked.

3. Camper Vans:

Camper vans, or Class B motorhomes, are compact and versatile vehicles that combine the convenience of a van with the amenities of a motorhome. These are ideal for those who prioritize mobility and ease of parking while still enjoying basic comforts on the road.

4. Truck Campers:

Truck campers are portable living units that fit into the bed of a pickup truck. They offer a compact and lightweight alternative to larger RVs, making them suitable for off-road adventures and reaching more remote locations. Truck campers typically feature sleeping quarters, a small kitchen, and bathroom facilities.

5. Pop-Up Trailers:

Pop-up trailers, also known as tent trailers or fold-down trailers, are lightweight towable units with collapsible sides. When parked, they expand to provide additional living space. Pop-up trailers are a budget-friendly option for those who enjoy the open-air camping experience with the added comfort of a trailer.

The diverse types of RVs available in the market cater to a broad spectrum of preferences, from those seeking the luxury of a Class A motorhome to adventurers who prefer the nimble and compact nature of camper vans or pop-up trailers. The variety ensures that there's an RV for every kind of traveler, making the open road accessible and enjoyable for all.

Book 1: Choosing the Right RV

Buying vs. Renting

(Photo of Foto di Kampus Production www.pexels.com)

The adventure of RV travel brings forth the pivotal decision of whether to buy or rent an RV. This choice is influenced by various factors, including one's travel frequency, financial considerations, and the desire for ownership versus the flexibility of renting. Each option, buying or renting, comes with its own set of pros and cons, making the decision a nuanced one that depends on individual preferences and circumstances.

Pros and Cons of Buying an RV:

Pros:

Ownership and Customization: One of the most significant advantages of buying an RV is ownership. When you purchase an RV, it becomes your personal vehicle, allowing for customization and personalization to suit your preferences. From interior modifications to exterior upgrades, owners have the freedom to tailor the RV to their liking.

Cost Savings in the Long Run: While the upfront cost of buying an RV can be substantial, especially for larger or more luxurious models, it can be more cost-effective in the long run for frequent travelers. Owning an RV eliminates rental fees, and with proper maintenance, the vehicle can provide years of travel at a lower cost per trip.

Spontaneity and Flexibility: RV owners have the freedom to embark on spontaneous trips without the need for reservations or adhering to rental schedules. This flexibility allows for a more carefree and adaptable travel experience, where the open road becomes a canvas for exploration.

Potential for Income Generation: Some RV owners choose to rent out their vehicles when not in use, turning their investment into a source of income. Peer-to-peer RV rental platforms have gained popularity, allowing owners to share the joy of RV travel while offsetting ownership costs.

Cons:

Upfront Cost and Depreciation: The initial investment required to purchase an RV, whether new or used, can be a significant financial commitment. Additionally, RVs depreciate over time, meaning their resale value may not match the initial purchase price.

Maintenance and Storage: Owning an RV involves ongoing maintenance costs, from regular servicing to potential repairs. Finding suitable storage, especially for larger RVs, can be a logistical challenge, and storage fees add to the overall cost of ownership.

Limited Model Variety: Once an RV is purchased, owners are committed to a specific model and type. Upgrading to a different model or type may require selling the existing RV, which can be a time-consuming process.

Pros and Cons of Renting an RV:

Pros:

Cost-Efficiency for Occasional Travelers: For those who plan to use an RV sporadically or for specific vacations, renting can be a cost-efficient option. Rental fees cover the duration of the trip, eliminating the need for a significant upfront investment.

Variety and Flexibility: Renting allows travelers to choose from a variety of RV types and models, tailoring the selection to the specific needs of each trip. This flexibility is advantageous, especially for individuals or families exploring different travel styles.

No Long-Term Commitment: Renting provides the freedom to enjoy RV travel without the long-term commitment associated with ownership. It is an excellent option for those who want to test the waters before deciding if RV travel is a lifestyle they want to fully embrace.

Reduced Maintenance Responsibilities: Renters are not burdened with the ongoing maintenance responsibilities that come with RV ownership. The rental agency typically handles maintenance and ensures the RV is in optimal condition for each trip.

Cons:

Limited Customization: Renters have limited control over the customization of the RV. While they can choose specific models, the interior and exterior features are generally standardized, limiting the personal touch that comes with ownership.

Scheduling Constraints: Renting an RV involves adhering to a set schedule, including pick-up and drop-off times. This can limit spontaneity and the ability to make impromptu changes to the travel itinerary.

Cumulative Rental Costs: For frequent travelers, the cumulative cost of renting an RV for multiple trips can surpass the initial investment of buying one. While renting is cost-efficient for occasional use, it may become less economical over time.

Availability and Booking Challenges: During peak travel seasons, securing a rental RV may pose challenges, especially for popular models or sizes. Planning well in advance is essential to ensure availability for desired travel dates.

Making the Decision:

Ultimately, the decision to buy or rent an RV hinges on individual preferences, travel frequency, and financial considerations. For those who relish the idea of ownership, customization, and the long-term potential for cost savings, buying an RV may be the preferred choice. On the other hand, renters seeking flexibility, variety, and a cost-efficient option for occasional trips may find that renting suits their needs better.

A hybrid approach is also gaining popularity, where individuals may choose to rent an RV for specific trips and circumstances, reserving ownership for those who want a consistent and personalized travel experience. This approach allows for flexibility while still enjoying the benefits of ownership when desired.

In conclusion, the decision to buy or rent an RV is a highly individualized one, influenced by lifestyle preferences, travel habits, and financial considerations. Both options open the door to the remarkable world of RV travel, where the journey itself becomes an adventure, regardless of the chosen mode of accommodation.

RV Features

Selecting the right Recreational Vehicle (RV) involves a careful consideration of size, amenities, and features to align with your travel preferences. The vast array of RV options available in the market can be overwhelming, but by understanding your specific needs and desires, you can ensure a comfortable and enjoyable journey. Let's explore key factors to consider when choosing the size, amenities, and features of an RV that best suit your travel style.

1. Choosing the Right Size:

Solo Travelers and Couples: For solo travelers or couples, compact RVs such as camper vans or Class B motorhomes may be ideal. These smaller vehicles offer maneuverability, easy parking, and are often equipped with all the necessary amenities for a cozy journey.

Families: Larger families may opt for Class C or Class A motorhomes with multiple sleeping areas and spacious interiors. Fifth-wheel trailers and conventional travel trailers are also popular choices, providing a variety of floor plans suitable for family travel.

Groups and Entertaining: If you plan to travel with a larger group or enjoy entertaining friends on the road, a Class A motorhome or a spacious travel trailer may be the best fit. These larger options often feature expansive living areas, kitchens, and multiple sleeping quarters.

Off-Road and Adventure: For those seeking off-road adventures or remote camping, compact options like truck campers or off-road trailers are designed for durability and versatility, allowing you to reach more secluded destinations.

2. Amenities for Comfort:

Sleeping Arrangements: Consider the number of people the RV needs to accommodate and the type of sleeping arrangements required. Some RVs offer private bedrooms with queen or king-sized beds, while others utilize convertible dining or living spaces for sleeping quarters.

Kitchen Facilities: Assess the kitchen amenities based on your cooking preferences. Larger RVs often feature full kitchens with stovetops, ovens, and spacious refrigerators, providing the convenience of preparing meals on the road. Smaller RVs may have compact kitchenettes suitable for simpler meal preparation.

Bathroom Facilities: Determine your preferences for bathroom facilities. Class A and Class C motorhomes typically feature full bathrooms with showers, while smaller RVs may have more compact wet baths or shared campground facilities.

Entertainment Systems: Consider the entertainment features that will enhance your travel experience. Many RVs come equipped with audiovisual systems, TVs, and even outdoor entertainment setups. Evaluate your preferences for entertainment and connectivity while on the road.

Heating and Cooling: Climate control is crucial for comfort during varying weather conditions. RVs are equipped with heating and cooling systems, ranging from air conditioning units to propane furnaces. Assess the efficiency of these systems to ensure a comfortable interior environment.

3. Specialized Features for Tailored Experiences:

Solar Power: For eco-conscious travelers or those planning to venture off the grid, RVs equipped with solar power systems provide sustainable energy solutions. Solar panels can charge batteries, allowing for increased self-sufficiency.

Outdoor Living Spaces: Some RVs feature exterior awnings, kitchens, or entertainment setups, creating additional living spaces outdoors. This is especially appealing for those who enjoy al fresco dining, relaxation, or hosting gatherings outside the RV.

Slide-Outs: Slide-out sections in RVs expand the interior living space when parked. This feature is common in larger RVs, providing a roomier feel without sacrificing maneuverability while driving.

Tech Connectivity: Consider the level of technology integration in the RV, especially if you plan to work remotely or rely on connectivity during your travels. Many modern RVs come equipped with Wi-Fi, USB ports, and smart home features.

Storage: Ample storage space is crucial for long journeys. Evaluate the storage options within the RV, including closets, cabinets, and external compartments. Dedicated storage for outdoor equipment and gear is particularly beneficial for adventure enthusiasts.

4. Budget Considerations:

New vs. Used: Decide whether a new or used RV aligns with your budget. While a new RV offers the latest features and warranties, a well-maintained used RV can provide cost savings without compromising on comfort.

Financing Options: Explore financing options, including loans and payment plans, to make RV ownership more accessible. Many financial institutions offer specialized RV financing with favorable terms.

Operating Costs: Beyond the initial purchase, consider the ongoing operating costs, including fuel, maintenance, insurance, and campground fees. Budgeting for these expenses ensures a realistic assessment of the overall cost of RV ownership.

Conclusion:

Choosing the right RV involves a thoughtful consideration of size, amenities, and features tailored to your travel preferences. Whether you prioritize comfort, adventure, or sustainability, the diverse options in the RV market provide a vehicle that aligns with your unique vision of the open road. By understanding your needs and desires, you can embark on a journey where the RV is not just a mode of transportation but a personalized haven that enhances the joy of travel.

Book 2: Planning Your RV Adventure

Route Planning

(Photo of Athena www.pexels.com)

An RV adventure across the vast landscapes of the United States requires thoughtful route planning to ensure a seamless and unforgettable journey. The process of selecting scenic stops, RV-friendly campgrounds, and noteworthy attractions is instrumental in creating a travel experience that goes beyond the destination itself. Here are some tips to guide you in planning the perfect route for your RV expedition.

1. Define Your Travel Goals and Preferences:

Scenic Beauty: Identify the type of scenery you want to experience. Whether it's the majestic mountains, tranquil coastal views, or expansive deserts, understanding your scenic preferences will shape your route.

Adventure vs. Relaxation: Determine if you prefer an adventure-packed itinerary with outdoor activities or a more relaxed journey with ample time for leisurely exploration and relaxation.

Cultural and Historical Interest: Consider your interest in cultural and historical sites. Plan stops that align with your desire to explore museums, historic landmarks, or local traditions.

2. Utilize Online Resources and Apps:

RV-Specific Apps: Leverage RV-specific apps that offer valuable information on campgrounds, RV-friendly routes, and points of interest. Apps like RV Trip Wizard, AllStays, and Campendium provide insights from fellow RV enthusiasts.

Online Forums and Communities: Engage with online RV communities and forums to gather firsthand experiences and recommendations from other travelers. These platforms offer valuable insights into hidden gems and off-the-beaten-path destinations.

Google Maps and Trip Planners: Use mapping tools like Google Maps to visualize your route and identify potential stops. Utilize trip planning features to estimate travel times and distances between destinations.

3. Consider RV-Friendly Campgrounds:

Full Hookup vs. Boondocking: Decide whether you prefer full-hookup campgrounds with amenities like electricity, water, and sewer, or if you're open to boondocking in more remote areas without these facilities.

Research Campground Reviews: Explore reviews and ratings of campgrounds to ensure they align with your expectations. Look for facilities that cater to RVs, such as pull-through sites, dump stations, and spacious sites for larger vehicles.

Reservations: Plan ahead and make reservations, especially during peak travel seasons. While spontaneity is part of the RV experience, having reservations ensures a secure spot, particularly in popular campgrounds.

4. Balance Driving Time and Stops:

Avoid Overplanning: While it's essential to have a general itinerary, avoid overplanning every detail. Leave room for spontaneity and serendipitous discoveries along the way.

Consider Driving Distances: Plan manageable driving distances each day to avoid fatigue and make time for exploration. RV travel is as much about the journey as it is about the destinations.

Account for Road Conditions: Be mindful of road conditions, construction, and potential detours. Stay informed about any travel advisories that may impact your route.

5. Explore Scenic Byways and Detours:

Scenic Byways: Incorporate scenic byways into your route for breathtaking views and unique experiences. The U.S. boasts numerous designated scenic byways, each offering a distinct landscape and cultural narrative.

Detours for Hidden Gems: Be open to detours that lead to hidden gems and local attractions. Some of the most memorable discoveries happen when you venture off the main route.

National and State Parks: Include visits to national and state parks along your route. These protected areas showcase the natural beauty and diverse ecosystems of the country.

6. Prioritize Must-See Attractions:

Bucket List Stops: Identify must-see attractions that align with your interests. Whether it's the Grand Canyon, the Pacific Coast Highway, or iconic cities, these bucket list stops add depth to your journey.

Local Events and Festivals: Check local event calendars for festivals, fairs, and cultural events happening along your route. Participating in local celebrations provides an authentic and immersive experience.

Historical Landmarks: Plan visits to historical landmarks that offer insights into the rich history of the regions you traverse. These landmarks add educational and cultural value to your RV adventure.

7. Budget Considerations:

Fuel Costs: Estimate fuel costs based on your route and the fuel efficiency of your RV. Consider fueling up at more affordable locations and explore fuel loyalty programs for potential savings.

Camping Fees: Budget for camping fees, taking into account the variety of campgrounds you plan to visit. Some campgrounds offer discounts for longer stays or memberships.

Attraction Fees: Research entrance fees for attractions and national parks. Some passes, like the America the Beautiful pass, provide access to multiple federal recreation sites.

8. Safety and Practical Considerations:

Weather Conditions: Stay informed about weather conditions along your route. Be prepared for changes in climate and consider seasonal variations when planning your itinerary.

Roadside Assistance: Ensure your RV insurance includes roadside assistance or consider obtaining a separate plan. This provides peace of mind in case of breakdowns or emergencies.

Medical Facilities: Be aware of the locations of medical facilities and pharmacies along your route. It's essential to have access to healthcare resources, especially for longer journeys.

Crafting the perfect RV route involves a balance of meticulous planning and an openness to spontaneity. By defining your travel goals, utilizing online resources, considering RV-friendly campgrounds, and exploring scenic byways, you can create a journey that resonates with your preferences and leaves you with cherished memories. RV travel is not just about reaching a destination; it's about embracing the adventure, discovering hidden gems, and savoring the joy of the open road.

Itinerary Flexibility

In the world of RV travel, where the open road beckons with promises of adventure and discovery, the art of spontaneity becomes a vital element of the journey. While planning an itinerary provides structure and direction, the true magic often happens when travelers embrace flexibility. The ability to deviate from a set plan, explore uncharted territories, and savor the unexpected moments along the way transforms a simple road trip into an extraordinary expedition. Here, we delve into the importance of cultivating an itinerary that welcomes spontaneity and celebrates the joy of the unknown.

1. The Allure of the Unknown:

Serendipitous Discoveries: The beauty of travel lies in the unforeseen gems waiting to be discovered. From charming roadside diners to hidden natural wonders, the unknown has a way of surprising and delighting those who venture off the beaten path.

Local Insights: Embracing flexibility allows travelers to tap into the wealth of local knowledge. Recommendations from residents, chance encounters with fellow travelers, and impromptu conversations unveil the authentic essence of each destination.

Adaptability to Conditions: Itinerary flexibility becomes particularly valuable when faced with unexpected weather conditions, road closures, or detours. Being adaptable allows travelers to navigate challenges with ease and turn detours into opportunities.

2. Cultivating Spontaneity:

Open-Ended Exploration: A flexible itinerary opens the door to open-ended exploration. Rather than adhering strictly to preplanned stops and timelines, travelers can follow their curiosity, allowing the journey to unfold naturally.

Change of Plans: Sometimes, the allure of a place may lead to a change of plans. A captivating landscape, a local event, or a recommendation from a fellow traveler can inspire a detour that adds depth and richness to the overall experience.

Freedom to Follow Passions: Flexibility allows travelers to indulge in their passions. Whether it's an unexpected hiking trail, a local art exhibit, or a spontaneous food festival, the freedom to follow personal interests enhances the journey.

3. Embracing the Journey, Not Just the Destination:

Appreciating Transitions: A flexible itinerary encourages travelers to appreciate the transitions between destinations. It's not just about reaching the final destination but savoring the diverse landscapes, small towns, and cultural nuances that shape the journey.

Unscheduled Stops: Some of the most memorable moments occur during unscheduled stops. Whether it's a picturesque viewpoint, a roadside fruit stand, or a historical marker, these unplanned moments contribute to the richness of the travel experience.

Connecting with Locals: Spontaneous exploration provides opportunities to connect with locals. From striking up conversations at a coffee shop to joining in local festivities, these interactions offer insights into the community and foster a deeper understanding of the places visited.

4. Preserving Peace of Mind:

Reducing Stress: A rigid itinerary can sometimes lead to stress if things don't go as planned. Embracing flexibility reduces stress, allowing travelers to focus on the joy of the journey rather than feeling constrained by a tight schedule.

Adapting to Preferences: Preferences may evolve during the journey. A flexible itinerary accommodates changes in interests, allowing travelers to linger in places they love or move on quickly from those that don't resonate.

Unexpected Opportunities: The unexpected often brings opportunities for unique experiences. Whether it's an invitation to a local event, a chance to join a guided tour, or an offer to explore a hidden trail, flexibility enables travelers to seize these spontaneous opportunities.

5. Tips for Balancing Planning and Flexibility:

Have a General Outline: While embracing flexibility, it's helpful to have a general outline of the route and key destinations. This provides a loose structure while leaving room for spontaneity.

Be Open to Recommendations: Welcome recommendations from locals, fellow travelers, and online communities. These insights can lead to hidden gems and enrich the overall travel experience.

Use Technology Wisely: Leverage technology for real-time information on road conditions, weather updates, and potential stops. Apps and online resources can enhance spontaneity while ensuring informed decision-making.

6. Celebrating the Unexpected:

Memorable Stories: Some of the most cherished travel stories stem from unexpected moments. Whether it's a chance encounter with wildlife, stumbling upon a vibrant local market, or witnessing a breathtaking sunset, these experiences become the heart of the journey.

Camaraderie Among Travelers: Flexibility fosters camaraderie among fellow travelers. Shared adventures, impromptu gatherings, and collaborative decision-making create a sense of community on the road.

Personal Growth: Embracing the unexpected fosters personal growth. Overcoming challenges, adapting to new environments, and navigating the unknown contribute to resilience and a deeper sense of self-discovery.

Conclusion:

In the tapestry of RV travel, where the road unfolds as a canvas of possibilities, itinerary flexibility emerges as the brushstroke that paints the most vivid and memorable moments. The beauty of the journey lies not just in the planned destinations but in the spontaneity that transforms each mile into an adventure. By cultivating an itinerary that welcomes the unexpected, travelers not only embark on a physical journey but also on a voyage of self-discovery, connection, and the sheer joy of embracing the unknown.

Book 3: RV Maintenance and Safety

Pre-Trip Checks

Embarking on an RV adventure is an exciting prospect, but ensuring a safe and smooth journey requires thorough pre-trip checks. A comprehensive inspection of your RV before hitting the open road is not only a matter of safety but also contributes to the overall enjoyment of your travel experience. From the engine to the living quarters, a well-executed pre-trip inspection ensures that all systems are in optimal condition. Here's a detailed checklist to guide you through the essential pre-trip checks for a worry-free RV journey.

1. Exterior Inspection:

Tires: Check tire pressure and tread depth. Ensure that all tires, including the spare, are in good condition. Look for signs of wear, cuts, or bulges.

Wheel Lug Nuts: Tighten wheel lug nuts to the recommended torque. Ensure that they are secure and not loose.

Brakes: Test the brakes for responsiveness. If you notice any unusual sounds or vibrations, consult a professional for further inspection.

Lights: Inspect all exterior lights, including headlights, taillights, brake lights, and turn signals. Replace any burnt-out bulbs.

Windows and Mirrors: Clean and check all windows and mirrors for cracks or damage. Adjust mirrors for proper visibility.

Roof and Seals: Inspect the roof for signs of leaks or damage. Check seals around vents, skylights, and windows. Repair or reseal as needed.

2. Engine and Mechanical Components:

Fluid Levels: Check engine oil, transmission fluid, brake fluid, coolant, and power steering fluid. Top off or replace fluids as needed.

Battery: Inspect the battery for corrosion and ensure that the connections are tight. Test the battery voltage and replace it if necessary.

Belts and Hoses: Check belts and hoses for wear, cracks, or signs of damage. Replace any components showing signs of deterioration.

Exhaust System: Inspect the exhaust system for leaks, rust, or damage. Ensure that the muffler and pipes are in good condition.

Air Filters: Replace air filters in the engine and cabin if they are dirty or clogged.

3. Interior Systems:

Appliances: Test all appliances, including the stove, oven, refrigerator, and microwave. Ensure that they operate correctly on the appropriate power sources.

Water Systems: Check for leaks in the plumbing system. Test faucets, showerheads, and toilets. Ensure the water pump is functioning properly.

Propane Systems: Check propane tanks for leaks and ensure that all connections are secure. Test propane appliances and detectors.

Electrical Systems: Test all interior lights, outlets, and switches. Check the electrical panel for tripped breakers and ensure the power cord is in good condition.

HVAC Systems: Test both heating and air conditioning systems to ensure they provide the desired temperature control.

4. Safety Equipment:

Smoke and Carbon Monoxide Detectors: Test and replace batteries in smoke and carbon monoxide detectors. Ensure they are functioning properly.

Fire Extinguisher: Check the pressure gauge on the fire extinguisher and ensure it is within the recommended range. Verify that the extinguisher is easily accessible.

Emergency Exits: Test emergency exits, including windows and doors. Ensure they open and close smoothly.

5. RV Chassis and Suspension:

Suspension Components: Inspect the suspension components, including shocks, springs, and stabilizers. Look for signs of wear or damage.

Steering System: Check the steering system for any unusual noises or play. Ensure that the steering wheel is properly aligned.

Chassis Lubrication: Lubricate chassis components as recommended by the manufacturer.

Alignment: Verify that the RV wheels are properly aligned to prevent uneven tire wear.

6. RV Exterior:

Awnings: Inspect awnings for tears, mold, or damage. Ensure that the awning operates smoothly.

Slides and Extensions: Test slide-outs and extensions to ensure they open and close properly. Check for any obstructions or signs of malfunction.

Stabilizing Jacks: Test stabilizing jacks to ensure they are functioning correctly. Lubricate as needed.

Exterior Storage Compartments: Check all exterior storage compartments for proper functioning and security. Lubricate hinges and locks.

7. Documentation and Permits:

Insurance and Registration: Ensure that your RV insurance and registration are up to date. Keep these documents readily accessible during your trip.

Permits and Passes: If your route includes toll roads or national parks, ensure that you have the necessary permits and passes.

Emergency Information: Keep a list of emergency contacts, including roadside assistance and RV service providers. Store this information in a easily accessible location.

8. Miscellaneous Checks:

Weight Distribution: Verify that your RV is properly loaded and that weight is evenly distributed. Pay attention to payload limits.

Towing Equipment: If towing a vehicle, check the hitch, tow bar, and safety cables. Ensure that brake lights and turn signals on the towed vehicle are functional.

Leveling System: Test the leveling system to ensure it operates correctly. Check for leaks or malfunctions.

Security Measures: Confirm that all security measures, such as locks and alarms, are in working order.

A comprehensive pre-trip inspection is a crucial step in ensuring the safety, reliability, and overall enjoyment of your RV journey. By meticulously checking all aspects of your RV, from the engine to the living quarters, you can address potential issues before they escalate. Incorporating this checklist into your pre-trip routine not only enhances the safety of your travels but also provides the peace of mind to fully immerse yourself in the wonders of the open road. Remember, a well-maintained RV is not just a vehicle; it's a reliable companion on your journey of exploration and adventure.

Basic Maintenance

To ensure a smooth and trouble-free journey, regular maintenance is key. Just like any vehicle, RVs require attention and care to keep all systems operating at their best. In this guide, we'll walk you through basic RV maintenance tasks and offer troubleshooting tips for common issues, empowering you to enjoy your travels with confidence.

1. Routine Inspection Checklist:

Roof: Regularly inspect the roof for signs of leaks, cracks, or damage. Check seams and seals around vents and other roof fixtures. Clean the roof at least twice a year to prevent the buildup of dirt and debris.

Exterior Seals: Check all exterior seals, including those around windows, doors, and compartments. Replace any damaged or deteriorated seals to prevent water infiltration.

Tires: Monitor tire pressure regularly, and check for signs of wear or damage. Rotate tires as recommended by the manufacturer. Ensure that the spare tire is in good condition.

Batteries: Inspect the batteries for corrosion and check the fluid levels if applicable. Clean battery terminals and connections. Consider using a battery tender to maintain charge during periods of inactivity.

Fluid Levels: Check engine oil, transmission fluid, brake fluid, coolant, and power steering fluid regularly. Top off or replace fluids as needed.

Brakes: Test the brakes for responsiveness. Inspect brake pads and discs for wear, and replace them if necessary. Bleed the brake lines if air is present.

Propane System: Regularly check propane tanks for leaks and ensure that all connections are tight. Test propane appliances to verify proper operation.

Safety Equipment: Test smoke detectors, carbon monoxide detectors, and fire extinguishers regularly. Replace batteries as needed and ensure that these safety devices are in good working order.

2. Interior Maintenance:

Appliances: Test all interior appliances, including the stove, oven, refrigerator, and microwave. Ensure that they operate correctly on the appropriate power sources.

Water Systems: Regularly check for leaks in the plumbing system. Test faucets, showerheads, and toilets. Ensure the water pump is functioning properly.

HVAC Systems: Test both heating and air conditioning systems to ensure they provide the desired temperature control. Replace filters as recommended by the manufacturer.

Seals and Gaskets: Check seals around windows and doors for wear and tear. Lubricate slide-out seals to prevent cracking and maintain flexibility.

Interior Cleanliness: Keep the interior clean and free of debris. Regularly clean carpets, upholstery, and surfaces to prevent the buildup of dirt and allergens.

3. Chassis and Suspension:

Suspension Components: Inspect the suspension components, including shocks, springs, and stabilizers. Look for signs of wear or damage. Lubricate moving parts as recommended.

Steering System: Check the steering system for any unusual noises or play. Ensure that the steering wheel is properly aligned.

Chassis Lubrication: Lubricate chassis components as recommended by the manufacturer. Grease fittings and joints to prevent excessive wear.

Alignment: Verify that the RV wheels are properly aligned to prevent uneven tire wear.

4. Exterior Care:

Awnings: Inspect awnings for tears, mold, or damage. Clean awnings regularly and ensure that they operate smoothly.

Slides and Extensions: Test slide-outs and extensions to ensure they open and close properly. Lubricate moving parts and check for any obstructions.

Stabilizing Jacks: Test stabilizing jacks to ensure they are functioning correctly. Lubricate as needed.

Exterior Storage Compartments: Regularly check all exterior storage compartments for proper functioning and security. Lubricate hinges and locks.

5. Electrical Systems:

Batteries: Inspect the house and chassis batteries regularly. Clean terminals and connections. Test and replace batteries if necessary.

Electrical Wiring: Visually inspect all electrical wiring for signs of wear or damage. Tighten loose connections and replace frayed or damaged wiring.

Power Cords: Inspect power cords for any damage or exposed wires. Replace cords if there are signs of wear.

Inverter and Converter: Test the inverter and converter to ensure they are converting power correctly. Monitor their performance to catch any issues early.

Common Troubleshooting Tips:

Fridge Not Cooling: Check if the fridge is level; an unlevel fridge may not cool properly. Verify that the power source (electricity, propane, or battery) is functioning. Clean the condenser coils and vents for better airflow.

Water Heater Issues: Check for air in the propane line and purge it by turning the water heater off and on. Ensure the water heater bypass valve is in the correct position. Clean the burner assembly and thermocouple.

Slide-Out Problems: Lubricate slide-out mechanisms regularly to prevent sticking. Check for debris or obstructions in the slide-out tracks. Ensure proper alignment and adjustment.

Leaky Roof: Inspect the roof for visible damage and cracks. Check seams and seals around vents and fixtures. Use RV roof sealant to repair small leaks.

Battery Drain: Investigate potential sources of battery drain, such as lights or appliances left on. Test the house and chassis batteries, and replace them if necessary. Consider installing a battery disconnect switch.

Propane Smell: If you detect a propane smell, turn off the propane supply immediately. Check for leaks using a propane leak detector. If you find a leak, repair it before using propane appliances.

Brake Issues: If you experience braking issues, check for low brake fluid levels, worn brake pads, or air in the brake lines. Consult a professional for further diagnosis and repair.

Generator Problems: Regularly exercise the generator to keep it in good working condition. If the generator is not starting, check the fuel level, oil level, and air filter. Ensure the spark plug is clean and properly gapped. If problems persist, consult the generator's manual or seek professional assistance.

Electrical Outages: If you experience electrical outages, check the circuit breakers in the RV's electrical panel. Reset any tripped breakers. Verify that the RV is properly connected to a power source. If using a generator, ensure it is functioning correctly.

Slide-Out Awning Issues: If your slide-out awning is not retracting or extending properly, check for obstructions in the awning's track. Ensure the fabric is not binding. Lubricate moving parts and inspect the awning arms for any damage.

Water Leaks: Address water leaks promptly to prevent interior damage. Inspect seals, seams, and windows for signs of wear or damage. Use RV sealant to patch small leaks. If the issue persists, consult a professional to identify and fix the source of the leak.

Tips for Efficient RV Maintenance:

Create a Schedule: Establish a routine maintenance schedule to ensure that all tasks are consistently performed. Regular maintenance helps prevent larger issues from developing.

Keep Records: Maintain a detailed record of all maintenance tasks, repairs, and replacements. This record serves as a valuable reference for tracking the RV's overall condition and performance.

Invest in Quality Products: Use high-quality RV-specific products for cleaning, lubrication, and sealant. Products designed for RV use are formulated to address the unique challenges of mobile living.

Learn DIY Basics: Familiarize yourself with basic DIY tasks, such as changing air filters, checking fluid levels, and lubricating moving parts. This knowledge empowers you to address minor issues on your own.

Regularly Exercise Components: Operate various components of your RV regularly, even during periods of inactivity. This includes running the generator, exercising slide-outs, and testing appliances to keep them in good working order.

Conduct Pre-Trip Checks: In addition to routine maintenance, perform thorough pre-trip checks before each journey. This ensures that your RV is in optimal condition for the upcoming adventure.

Be Proactive: Address issues promptly rather than delaying repairs. Proactive maintenance prevents small problems from escalating into major, more costly issues.

Join RV Communities: Engage with RV communities, forums, and online groups to exchange maintenance tips, share experiences, and seek advice from seasoned RV enthusiasts.

Consider Professional Inspections: Periodically, consider having your RV professionally inspected. An experienced technician can identify potential issues that may not be apparent during routine checks.

Prepare for Seasonal Changes: Adjust your maintenance routine based on seasonal changes. Winterization is crucial for protecting your RV in colder climates, while summer maintenance may focus on cooling systems and awnings.

Store Properly: If storing your RV for an extended period, choose a suitable storage location. Ensure the RV is clean, and all perishables are removed to prevent attracting pests. Use RV covers for added protection.

Conclusion:

Regular RV maintenance is the key to a reliable and enjoyable travel experience. By incorporating routine inspections, addressing issues promptly, and staying proactive in your approach, you'll not only enhance the longevity of your RV but also minimize the likelihood of unexpected breakdowns. Whether you're a seasoned RV enthusiast or a newcomer to the world of mobile living, embracing a thorough maintenance routine ensures that your RV remains a dependable companion on your journey of exploration and adventure. With proper care, your RV becomes more than just a vehicle—it becomes a portal to new destinations and unforgettable experiences.

(Photo of Luk www.pexels.com)

Book 4: Navigating RV Parks and Campgrounds

Choosing Campgrounds

Selecting the right campgrounds and RV parks is a crucial aspect of planning a successful and enjoyable RV journey. The places where you choose to rest, relax, and connect with fellow travelers can significantly impact your overall experience. From amenities to location, each factor plays a role in determining the suitability of a campground for your specific needs. In this guide, we'll explore the key considerations when choosing campgrounds, empowering you to navigate the vast array of options and find your ideal home on the road.

1. Campground Amenities:

Full Hookups: Campgrounds offering full hookups provide connections for water, electricity, and sewer. This convenience allows for a more comfortable and self-sufficient RV experience.

Electrical Service: Ensure the campground provides the appropriate electrical service for your RV. Common options include 30-amp and 50-amp hookups. Verify the compatibility of your RV's electrical system with the campground's offerings.

Wi-Fi and Connectivity: In an increasingly connected world, access to Wi-Fi can be a valuable amenity. Check if the campground provides reliable internet connectivity, especially if you rely on it for work or entertainment.

Laundry Facilities: On longer journeys, access to laundry facilities can be a significant convenience. Look for campgrounds that offer clean and well-maintained laundry areas.

Restrooms and Showers: Clean and accessible restrooms and showers are essential for a comfortable stay. Check reviews or inquire about the campground's restroom facilities before making a reservation.

Recreation Areas: Consider your recreational preferences. Some campgrounds offer amenities such as swimming pools, playgrounds, hiking trails, or organized activities. Choose a campground that aligns with your interests and preferences for downtime activities.

Pet-Friendly Policies: If you travel with pets, confirm the campground's pet policies. Look for pet-friendly amenities such as dog parks or walking trails. Ensure that your pets are welcome and that the campground enforces responsible pet ownership.

2. Location and Scenery:

Proximity to Attractions: Consider the proximity of the campground to attractions, national parks, or points of interest you plan to visit. A conveniently located campground can enhance the efficiency of your travel itinerary.

Scenic Views: If you enjoy waking up to scenic views or want to witness breathtaking sunsets, choose campgrounds with picturesque surroundings. Waterfront locations, mountain vistas, or wooded landscapes can provide a beautiful backdrop for your RV adventure.

Accessibility: Evaluate the accessibility of the campground, especially if you have a larger RV or specific accessibility requirements. Check for ease of entry, maneuverability within the campground, and the availability of pull-through sites.

Weather Considerations: Depending on the time of year and your travel route, consider the local climate and weather conditions. Some campgrounds may have seasonal closures, and extreme weather can impact your comfort and safety.

Quietness and Privacy: Assess the level of privacy and noise at the campground. If you prefer a quieter environment, choose campgrounds that prioritize tranquility and offer well-spaced sites.

3. Campground Reviews and Ratings:

Online Platforms: Utilize online platforms and campground review websites to gather insights from fellow RV enthusiasts. Reviews often provide valuable information about the cleanliness, amenities, and overall experience at a campground.

Social Media Groups: Join RV-specific social media groups or forums to connect with other travelers. Seek recommendations and firsthand experiences from those who have stayed at campgrounds along your planned route.

Campground Memberships: Consider joining campground membership programs, such as Good Sam Club or KOA Rewards, which offer discounts, member-only deals, and a network of affiliated campgrounds.

Word of Mouth: Personal recommendations from friends, family, or fellow RVers can be invaluable. Ask for suggestions and tips from those who have explored similar routes or destinations.

4. Cost Considerations:

Daily Rates: Compare the daily rates of different campgrounds to ensure they align with your budget. Rates can vary based on location, amenities, and the time of year.

Discount Programs: Explore discount programs, loyalty programs, or memberships that offer reduced rates for campground stays. Some programs provide discounts for extended stays or loyalty points for future use.

Cancellation Policies: Review the campground's cancellation policies. Life on the road can be unpredictable, and flexible cancellation policies provide peace of mind in case plans need to change.

Additional Fees: Inquire about additional fees, such as pet fees, resort fees, or amenity-specific charges. Understanding the full cost of your stay helps avoid surprises.

5. Size and Type of Campground:

RV Size Restrictions: Some campgrounds have size restrictions, limiting the length or type of RVs they can accommodate. Verify that the campground can accommodate the size and type of your RV.

Campground Type: Choose a campground that aligns with your preferences. Options include private campgrounds, public campgrounds (state or national parks), RV resorts, and boondocking locations. Each type offers a different experience, from luxury amenities to rustic wilderness camping.

Availability of Reservations: Determine if the campground accepts reservations, especially during peak travel seasons. Reserving in advance ensures you have a guaranteed spot, especially in popular destinations.

Community Atmosphere: Consider the atmosphere of the campground. Some campgrounds emphasize community and social activities, while others cater to a quieter and more private experience.

6. Regulations and Policies:

Length of Stay Limits: Check if the campground has any restrictions on the length of stay. Some campgrounds may have maximum stay limits, especially during peak seasons.

Generator Hours: Be aware of generator usage policies. Some campgrounds may have specific hours during which generators can be operated, while others may allow continuous use.

Quiet Hours: Respect quiet hours to ensure a peaceful atmosphere for all campers. Familiarize yourself with the campground's quiet hours and adhere to them.

Waste Disposal Policies: Understand the campground's waste disposal policies, including rules for graywater and blackwater disposal. Some campgrounds may require the use of designated dump stations.

7. Seasonal Considerations:

Peak Seasons: Be mindful of peak travel seasons, especially in popular tourist destinations. Campgrounds may be busier, and reservations may fill up quickly during these times. Plan ahead to secure your preferred spots.

Off-Peak Benefits: Consider exploring off-peak seasons for a more tranquil experience. Many campgrounds offer discounted rates during shoulder seasons, providing an opportunity to enjoy popular destinations with fewer crowds.

8. Environmental Impact:

Leave No Trace: Embrace Leave No Trace principles to minimize your environmental impact. Choose campgrounds that promote responsible camping practices, and follow guidelines for waste disposal, recycling, and conservation.

Boondocking: For those seeking a closer connection to nature, boondocking or dispersed camping in designated areas allows you to camp off the grid. Be sure to research and adhere to regulations regarding dispersed camping in specific regions.

9. Connectivity Needs:

Remote Work Considerations: If you're a digital nomad or require internet access for work, prioritize campgrounds with reliable connectivity. Check online reviews for information on the quality of Wi-Fi or cellular service at the campground.

Digital Detox: Conversely, if you're looking for a break from technology, consider campgrounds in more remote locations where connectivity may be limited. This allows you to fully immerse yourself in the natural surroundings.

10. Community and Events:

Community Engagement: Some campgrounds foster a strong sense of community through organized events and activities. If you enjoy socializing with fellow travelers, look for campgrounds with communal spaces and scheduled gatherings.

Themed Events: Some campgrounds host themed events or festivals. Whether it's a music festival, a culinary event, or outdoor workshops, these can add an extra layer of enjoyment to your stay.

11. Safety and Security:

Campground Security: Prioritize safety by choosing campgrounds with visible security measures. Well-lit areas, security personnel, and gated access contribute to a secure environment for you and your belongings.

Emergency Services: Familiarize yourself with the proximity of emergency services, including hospitals and service stations, in case of unforeseen circumstances. Ensure that campground staff can provide assistance if needed.

12. Repeat Experiences:

Favorite Campgrounds: As you accumulate RV travel experience, you may discover favorite campgrounds that align perfectly with your preferences. Consider returning to these beloved spots for a sense of familiarity and comfort.

Building a Routine: For long-term RVers or those seeking a routine, finding campgrounds that offer extended stay options or monthly rates can contribute to a more settled and predictable lifestyle.

Final Thoughts:

Choosing campgrounds for your RV journey is a dynamic and personal process, reflecting the uniqueness of your travel aspirations and lifestyle. By carefully weighing factors such as amenities, location, and community atmosphere, you can curate a list of campgrounds that align with your vision of the perfect RV adventure. Whether you prefer the tranquility of nature, the camaraderie of a vibrant community, or a blend of both, the diverse array of campgrounds across the country provides endless opportunities for exploration and discovery. With each carefully selected campground, your RV adventure becomes a tailored and unforgettable experience, turning the road into a canvas for your personal journey of discovery.

Etiquette

An RV adventure not only involves choosing the right campgrounds but also entails cultivating positive interactions within the RV community. Campground etiquette is the unwritten code that fosters a sense of community and ensures that everyone can enjoy their outdoor experiences to the fullest. Whether you're a seasoned RVer or new to the lifestyle, adhering to etiquette guidelines contributes to a harmonious and enjoyable environment for all. In this guide, we'll explore key aspects of campground etiquette and offer tips for being a considerate neighbor.

1. Respect Quiet Hours:

Understanding Quiet Hours: Most campgrounds have designated quiet hours during which loud activities and excessive noise should be minimized. Typically, quiet hours are in the evening and early morning. Familiarize yourself with the specific hours of the campground and be respectful of your neighbors' need for peace and quiet.

Generator Usage: If your RV is equipped with a generator, be mindful of when and how you use it. Some campgrounds have specific hours for generator operation. Avoid running generators during quiet hours unless it's a necessity, and position the exhaust away from neighboring RVs.

2. Keep Pets Well-Behaved:

Leash Rules: Always keep pets on a leash when outside your RV, even if the campground allows off-leash activities in designated areas. This helps prevent unexpected encounters and ensures the safety and comfort of other campers.

Clean Up After Pets: Always clean up after your pets. Carry waste bags and promptly dispose of pet waste in designated receptacles. Maintaining cleanliness is not only courteous but also essential for the well-being of the campground environment.

Respect Allergies and Fears: Be aware that not everyone is comfortable around pets, and some may have allergies or fears. Respect others' space and be considerate of their feelings. If your pet is particularly lively or social, be attentive to how they interact with others.

3. Observe Site Boundaries:

Respect Personal Space: RV sites are typically designed to provide a reasonable amount of personal space. Be mindful of your neighbors' privacy and avoid encroaching on their designated area. Respect site boundaries, including utility hookups and shared spaces.

Navigating Common Areas: Shared facilities like picnic tables, fire pits, and common areas are meant for communal use. If these spaces are not exclusive to your site, be considerate of others who may also want to utilize them.

Vehicle Parking: Park your vehicles within your designated space and avoid parking in a way that obstructs neighboring sites or common thoroughfares. Proper parking ensures smooth traffic flow and prevents inconvenience to others.

4. Manage Exterior Lighting:

Adequate Exterior Lighting: While exterior lighting is essential for safety and security, it's crucial to manage its intensity. Avoid overly bright lights that may disturb neighbors during nighttime hours. Consider using motion-sensor lights for added convenience.

Direct Lighting Downward: Point exterior lights downward to minimize light pollution. This not only benefits your immediate neighbors but also contributes to a more serene night environment for the entire campground.

Nighttime Navigation: If you need to move around your RV during the night, use a flashlight or headlamp to navigate instead of relying on bright exterior lights. This minimizes disturbances for nearby campers who may be trying to sleep.

5. Practice Fire Safety:

Campfire Considerations: If campfires are allowed, maintain a safe and controlled fire. Follow campground guidelines for fire pits, ensuring that fires are not excessively large or producing excessive smoke. Never leave a fire unattended.

Smoking Etiquette: If you smoke, do so in designated areas and dispose of cigarette butts properly. Avoid smoking near common areas, other RVs, or where smoke might drift into neighboring sites.

Firewood Use: Use only approved firewood and follow campground rules regarding firewood collection and transport. Invasive pests and diseases can be spread through improperly sourced firewood.

6. Observe Waste Disposal Guidelines:

Proper Garbage Disposal: Dispose of trash in designated receptacles provided by the campground. Ensure that garbage bags are securely tied to prevent spills or odors. If recycling facilities are available, separate recyclables from general waste.

Dump Station Etiquette: Use dump stations for graywater and blackwater disposal, and follow proper procedures to avoid spills and contamination. Be patient and allow others to use the dump station efficiently.

Minimize Noise During Cleanup: If you're breaking camp early in the morning, be mindful of noise levels during the process. Avoid slamming doors, loud conversations, or running engines excessively.

7. Maintain a Tidy Campsite:

Outdoor Storage: Keep outdoor storage organized and tidy. Avoid leaving items such as chairs, mats, or hoses scattered around your site, especially in shared spaces.

Awning and Slide-Out Considerations: When extending awnings or slide-outs, ensure that they don't encroach on neighboring sites. Be aware of the overall footprint of your RV setup to maintain harmony with the surrounding environment.

Respect Natural Elements: Avoid damaging or disturbing natural elements, such as plants and trees, within your campsite. Many campgrounds strive to preserve natural landscapes, and respecting these elements contributes to the overall beauty of the area.

8. Follow Pet and Wildlife Guidelines:

Wildlife Interaction: Resist the temptation to feed or approach wildlife. Feeding wildlife can disrupt natural behaviors and poses risks to both animals and campers.

Secure Food and Trash: Store food securely to prevent attracting wildlife to your campsite. This includes properly sealing food containers, using bear-resistant containers if necessary, and keeping trash in sealed bags.

Prevent Pet Disturbances: Ensure that your pets do not disturb wildlife or other campers. Keep them on a leash when in areas where wildlife may be present, and do not allow them to chase or harass animals.

9. Be Considerate of Generators:

Generator Use During Quiet Hours: Avoid using generators during designated quiet hours, as the noise can disturb neighboring campers. If you need to run a generator for essential purposes, communicate with nearby campers and seek their understanding.

Proper Placement: Position your generator in a way that directs exhaust away from neighboring RVs. This minimizes the impact of noise and fumes on others.

Monitor Noise Levels: Generators produce noise, even during permitted hours. Be mindful of the noise levels and consider using quieter generator models if possible.

10. Communicate and Collaborate:

Friendly Communication: Foster a friendly atmosphere by greeting your neighbors and engaging in courteous conversations. A simple greeting and introduction can go a long way in building positive connections within the RV community.

Address Concerns Directly: If you encounter any issues or concerns with neighboring campers, address them directly and respectfully. Open communication allows for a quick resolution and prevents the escalation of minor disputes.

Assist Others: Be willing to offer assistance or guidance to fellow campers, especially newcomers. Whether it's sharing tips on RV maintenance or helping with setup, a spirit of helpfulness enhances the overall campground experience for everyone.

Conclusion:

Campground etiquette is the cornerstone of a positive and harmonious RV community. By adhering to these unwritten rules, you contribute to a welcoming environment where campers can enjoy the beauty of nature, forge connections, and create lasting memories. As you embark on your RV adventures, keep in mind that every camper plays a role in shaping the collective experience. A considerate and respectful approach to campground etiquette not only enhances your own journey but also contributes to the overall well-being and enjoyment of the RV community. Embrace the spirit of camaraderie, be mindful of your impact on the environment, and treasure the opportunity to connect with fellow travelers on the road less traveled. In practicing campground etiquette, you not only become a considerate neighbor but also a positive ambassador for the vibrant and diverse RV lifestyle.

Book 5: Living Comfortably in Your RV

Packing Essentials

(Photo of Kampus Production www.pexels.com)

RV adventure offers the promise of freedom, exploration, and a unique lifestyle on the open road. However, the key to truly savoring this nomadic existence lies in the art of efficient packing. Living comfortably in your RV demands a thoughtful selection of essentials, kitchen supplies, outdoor gear, and more. In this guide, we'll delve into creating a comprehensive packing checklist to ensure you have everything you need for a comfortable and enjoyable journey.

1. Essentials:

Documentation: Carry all necessary documents, including your driver's license, registration for the RV, insurance information, and any required permits for your journey.

Medical Kit: Assemble a well-stocked first aid kit with basic medications, bandages, antiseptics, and any prescription medications you may need.

Emergency Contacts: Keep a list of emergency contacts, including roadside assistance, RV service centers, and local emergency services.

2. Kitchen Supplies:

Cookware: Opt for versatile and compact cookware such as a set of pots and pans with nesting capabilities. Consider non-stick options for easy cleaning.

Cutlery and Utensils: Pack a set of knives, spatulas, ladles, and other essential utensils. Don't forget items like can openers, bottle openers, and kitchen scissors.

Dishes and Flatware: Choose durable and lightweight dishes, bowls, and flatware. Consider stackable options to optimize storage space.

Coffee Maker or Kettle: If you're a coffee enthusiast, bring a compact coffee maker or kettle for your daily caffeine fix.

Food Storage Containers: Use a variety of sizes for storing leftovers, prepped ingredients, and snacks. Collapsible containers are ideal for saving space.

Basic Pantry Items: Stock up on essential pantry items such as spices, oils, condiments, and other non-perishables. Consider space-saving spice containers.

Cleaning Supplies: Pack dish soap, sponges, kitchen towels, and trash bags. Opt for biodegradable and eco-friendly cleaning products when possible.

3. Bedding and Linens:

Sheets and Pillowcases: Bring a set of comfortable sheets and pillowcases suitable for your RV bed size. Consider moisture-wicking materials for better comfort.

Blankets and Comforters: Depending on the climate, pack blankets or comforters to stay warm during cooler nights.

Towels: Have a mix of bath towels, hand towels, and washcloths. Quick-dry towels are convenient for RV living.

Mattress Topper: Enhance sleeping comfort with a mattress topper. Choose one that is easily foldable or rollable for efficient storage.

Laundry Bag: Keep a laundry bag to collect dirty clothes. Choose a breathable and collapsible option.

4. Clothing and Personal Items:

Weather-Appropriate Clothing: Pack clothing suitable for various weather conditions, including lightweight options for hot climates and layered items for colder regions.

Footwear: Bring comfortable and versatile footwear for different activities, including walking shoes, sandals, and possibly hiking boots.

Toiletries: Assemble a compact toiletry kit with essentials like toothbrush, toothpaste, shampoo, conditioner, soap, and any personal care items you use regularly.

Medications and First Aid: Ensure you have an ample supply of prescription medications. Replenish your first aid kit with any necessary items.

5. Outdoor and Recreational Gear:

Camping Chairs: Comfortable and foldable camping chairs are perfect for outdoor relaxation.

Portable Grill: Enjoy outdoor cooking with a portable grill. Choose one that is compact and easy to store.

Outdoor Table: A collapsible table is handy for dining or setting up outdoor activities.

Hiking Gear: If you enjoy hiking, pack appropriate footwear, backpacks, and other gear for your outdoor adventures.

Biking Equipment: If you plan to explore on bikes, bring helmets, bike racks, and any necessary tools for maintenance.

6. RV Maintenance and Tools:

Basic Toolkit: Include essential tools for minor RV repairs and maintenance, such as screwdrivers, pliers, wrenches, and a multi-tool.

Tire Maintenance: Carry a tire pressure gauge, a jack, and any necessary tools for changing a flat tire.

Leveling Blocks: Ensure your RV is level at your campsite by bringing leveling blocks.

Sewer Hose and Accessories: Have a high-quality sewer hose and necessary accessories for waste disposal.

Water Hoses and Filters: Pack hoses for fresh water hookup, along with water filters to ensure clean water supply.

Electrical Adapters: Bring adapters to connect to various types of electrical hookups at campgrounds and RV parks. Verify the power requirements of your RV and have the appropriate adapters for different amp services.

7. Entertainment and Electronics:

Books and Magazines: If you enjoy reading, bring a selection of books or magazines for leisurely moments.

Board Games and Cards: Pack compact board games or a deck of cards for entertaining evenings with friends or family.

Electronics Chargers: Ensure you have chargers for all your electronic devices, including phones, tablets, laptops, and cameras.

Portable Power Bank: A portable power bank can be a lifesaver when electrical hookups are not available.

8. Miscellaneous Items:

Folding Tables and Chairs: Additional folding tables and chairs can be useful for hosting guests or setting up workstations.

Rugs or Mats: Outdoor rugs or mats can define your outdoor living space and help keep dirt out of the RV.

Collapsible Storage Bins: Use collapsible storage bins to keep items organized and maximize storage space.

Trash and Recycling Bins: Portable and compact trash and recycling bins are essential for maintaining a clean and eco-friendly RV space.

9. Safety and Security:

Smoke and Carbon Monoxide Detectors: Ensure your RV is equipped with working smoke and carbon monoxide detectors.

Fire Extinguisher: Keep a readily accessible fire extinguisher in case of emergencies.

Emergency Kit: Assemble an emergency kit with essentials like flashlights, batteries, a multi-tool, and a basic first aid kit.

RV Security System: Consider installing a security system for added protection when parked at campgrounds or boondocking.

10. Personal Comfort Items:

Favorite Snacks: Bring a selection of your favorite snacks to satisfy cravings on the road.

Comfortable Seating: Consider adding cushions or seat covers to enhance the comfort of your RV's seating.

Adequate Lighting: Invest in LED lights or string lights to create a cozy and well-lit atmosphere inside and outside the RV.

Decorative Touches: Personalize your RV space with small decorations or items that bring you joy.

11. Cleaning and Maintenance Supplies:

Cleaning Products: Bring RV-friendly cleaning products for maintaining a tidy living space.

Broom and Dustpan: Keep a compact broom and dustpan for quick cleanups.

Lubricants and WD-40: Have lubricants and WD-40 for addressing squeaky or stiff components in and around the RV.

Disposable Gloves: Disposable gloves are handy for messier tasks, such as waste disposal or handling dirty items.

12. Organization and Storage Solutions:

Storage Baskets and Bins: Utilize storage baskets and bins to keep items organized in cabinets and closets.

Over-the-Door Hooks: Maximize storage by using over-the-door hooks for towels, hats, or other accessories.

Hanging Shelves: Hanging shelves inside closets or cabinets provide additional storage for clothing or smaller items.

Vacuum Sealer: Consider a vacuum sealer for preserving food and optimizing storage space in the refrigerator.

13. Personal Technology:

Portable Wi-Fi Hotspot: A portable Wi-Fi hotspot ensures connectivity in areas with weak signals.

GPS Navigation: Use a reliable GPS navigation system or navigation apps for seamless travel planning.

Entertainment Streaming: If you enjoy streaming, consider a portable device for accessing your favorite shows and movies.

14. Seasonal and Destination-Specific Items:

Winter Gear: If traveling in colder climates, bring winter gear such as thermal clothing, blankets, and heated blankets.

Beach Gear: For coastal destinations, pack beach essentials like swimsuits, sunscreen, and beach chairs.

Camping Equipment: If planning to boondock or camp in remote areas, bring camping equipment such as tents, sleeping bags, and portable stoves.

15. Regular RV Maintenance Schedule:

Checklist for Routine Maintenance: Develop a checklist for regular RV maintenance tasks, including checking fluid levels, inspecting the roof, and cleaning filters.

Scheduled Inspections: Plan for scheduled inspections of the RV's systems, appliances, and overall condition.

Pre-Trip Checks: Before each journey, conduct pre-trip checks to ensure everything is in working order.

Conclusion:

Efficient packing is the cornerstone of a comfortable and enjoyable RV lifestyle. By meticulously curating your packing list and staying organized, you'll create a home on wheels that meets your needs and preferences. As you embark on your RV adventure, remember that flexibility is key, and your packing strategy may evolve based on your experiences. Embrace the freedom of the open road, savor the simplicity of RV living, and ensure that your journey is filled with moments of joy, discovery, and lasting memories.

Organization Tips

Living in an RV presents a unique challenge: making the most of limited space while maintaining comfort and functionality. With thoughtful organization, you can transform your compact living quarters into an efficient and clutter-free haven. Here are some organizational hacks to maximize space inside your RV:

1. Multi-Functional Furniture:

Invest in furniture that serves multiple purposes. For example, choose a sofa that can convert into a bed or an ottoman with hidden storage space. Folding tables and chairs are also excellent space-saving options.

2. Vertical Storage Solutions:

Utilize vertical space by installing shelves, hooks, and hanging organizers. Mount shelves on walls for items like books, plants, or decorative pieces. Hooks can hold kitchen utensils, towels, or hats, and hanging organizers are perfect for shoes, toiletries, or accessories.

3. Collapsible and Stackable Containers:

Opt for collapsible containers for items like laundry baskets, storage bins, and dishware. When not in use, these containers can be flattened or stacked, minimizing the space they occupy.

4. Over-the-Door Organizers:

Install over-the-door organizers on bathroom and closet doors. These organizers are ideal for storing toiletries, shoes, accessories, or even kitchen supplies. They keep essentials easily accessible while freeing up valuable counter and cabinet space.

5. Drawer Dividers and Organizers:

Keep drawers tidy with dividers and organizers. These accessories prevent items from shifting during travel and make it easier to find what you need. Consider adjustable dividers to accommodate various-sized items.

6. Hanging Shoe Organizers in Cabinets:

Repurpose hanging shoe organizers by placing them inside cabinets or closets. This creative solution provides pockets for storing small items like cleaning supplies, snacks, or toiletries without cluttering valuable counter space.

7. Rolling Cart for Kitchen Storage:

Integrate a rolling cart in the kitchen for additional storage and workspace. This portable solution can hold kitchen appliances, utensils, or pantry items. When not in use, it can be rolled away to create more floor space.

8. Magnetic Spice Racks:

Maximize kitchen cabinet space by using magnetic spice racks. Attach these racks to the inside of cabinet doors to store spices, condiments, or small kitchen tools. This keeps the countertops clear and enhances accessibility.

9. Under-Bed Storage:

Take advantage of the space under the bed for storage. Use bins or drawers that can slide in and out easily. This area is perfect for stowing away seasonal clothing, shoes, or items you don't need daily.

10. Cabinet Door Caddies:

Install caddies on the inside of cabinet doors to hold items like cutting boards, baking sheets, or cleaning supplies. This clever use of vertical space ensures that commonly used items are within reach without cluttering countertops.

11. Magnetic Knife Strips:

Save counter space by installing magnetic knife strips on the walls. This not only organizes knives but can also be used for metal utensils, keys, or other magnetic items.

12. Fold-Down Tables:

Install fold-down tables in dining or work areas. These tables can be secured to the wall and easily folded when not in use, providing extra room for activities and movement.

13. Under-Cabinet Hooks:

Attach hooks under cabinets to hang mugs, cups, or utensils. This prevents the need for additional cupboards and adds a touch of functionality to your kitchen space.

14. Mesh Netting or Bungee Cords:

Secure loose items with mesh netting or bungee cords. These can be used in cabinets or storage compartments to prevent items from shifting during travel.

15. Labeling Systems:

Implement a labeling system for containers and bins. Clearly labeling items makes it easier to find what you need quickly and helps maintain an organized living space.

In the confined quarters of an RV, every inch counts. By embracing these organizational hacks, you can transform your RV into a well-ordered and efficient space where everything has its place. From maximizing vertical storage to repurposing everyday items, these tips ensure that you make the most of your RV's limited space without sacrificing comfort or convenience.

Book 6: Budgeting for RV Travel

Cost Breakdown

It's essential to be well-versed in the costs associated with RV travel to plan and budget effectively. The expenses encompass various aspects, including fuel, campgrounds, maintenance, and additional considerations that contribute to the overall cost of this unique mode of exploration.

1. Fuel Costs:

One of the primary expenses for RV travel is fuel. The cost varies based on factors such as the size of the RV, the type of fuel it uses, and the distance traveled. Larger Class A motorhomes typically have lower fuel efficiency compared to smaller Class B or C models. To estimate fuel costs, consider the average miles per gallon (MPG) of your RV and the current fuel prices along your route.

2. Campground Fees:

Campground fees are a significant component of RV travel expenses. The cost varies depending on the type of campground, amenities offered, and the region. Campground options include public parks, private RV parks, and boondocking (free camping on public lands). Public parks often offer lower fees, while private RV parks may provide additional amenities like hookups, Wi-Fi, and recreational facilities at a higher cost. Boondocking, while economical, may require additional investments in equipment for self-sufficiency.

3. Maintenance and Repairs:

Maintaining an RV is crucial for a safe and enjoyable journey. Budget for regular maintenance tasks such as oil changes, tire rotations, and brake inspections. Additionally, allocate funds for unexpected repairs or emergencies. The age and condition of the RV can influence maintenance costs, so having a contingency fund for unforeseen issues is advisable.

4. Insurance Premiums:

RV insurance is essential for protecting your investment and covering potential liabilities. Insurance premiums vary based on factors like the type of RV, coverage options, and your driving history. Liability coverage, comprehensive coverage, and collision coverage are common components of RV insurance. It's recommended to shop around for insurance quotes to find the best coverage at a reasonable cost.

5. Depreciation:

While not a direct out-of-pocket expense, depreciation is a consideration for long-term RV owners. RVs, like vehicles, depreciate over time. Understanding the depreciation rate of your RV model is essential for gauging its resale value. While depreciation is inevitable, maintaining the RV in good condition and staying updated on regular maintenance can mitigate its impact.

6. Tolls and Road Fees:

Tolls and road fees are often overlooked but can accumulate, especially when traversing toll roads or crossing certain bridges. Plan your routes and be aware of tolls along the way to include them in your travel budget.

7. RV Storage:

For those who don't use their RVs year-round, storage costs can be a consideration. Whether storing the RV during the off-season or between trips, factor in storage fees when calculating the overall cost of RV ownership.

8. RV Accessories and Upgrades:

Personalizing your RV with accessories and upgrades is part of the RV lifestyle. While not mandatory, these additions can enhance comfort and convenience. Budget for items such as outdoor furniture, grills, solar panels, or technology upgrades based on your preferences and needs.

9. Entertainment and Activities:

Beyond the basic necessities, allocate funds for entertainment and activities. Explore local attractions, attend events, or participate in recreational activities along your route. Budgeting for these experiences adds an extra layer of enjoyment to your RV adventure.

10. Dining Out and Groceries:

While RV travel allows for cooking your meals, dining out can be part of the experience. Budget for occasional restaurant meals or local culinary experiences. Additionally, allocate funds for groceries and supplies, especially if you plan to cook in your RV to save on dining expenses.

11. Communication and Connectivity:

Staying connected on the road may involve expenses related to internet connectivity, mobile plans, or campground Wi-Fi fees. Consider these costs to maintain communication, especially if you're a digital nomad or rely on internet access for remote work.

12. RV Club Memberships:

Joining RV clubs or memberships can provide access to discounts on campgrounds, fuel, and other services. While there may be an upfront cost for membership, the potential savings over time can make these memberships cost-effective for frequent RV travelers.

13. Healthcare and Insurance:

Don't overlook healthcare and insurance costs while on the road. Ensure that your health insurance provides coverage in various states, and consider travel insurance for added protection during your RV journey.

14. Licensing and Registration:

Licensing and registration fees for RVs vary by state. Research the requirements and associated costs for the states you plan to visit. Be aware of renewal dates to avoid late fees.

15. Resale Considerations:

If you envision selling your RV in the future, factor in costs related to preparing the RV for resale, advertising, and potential repairs or upgrades to increase its market value.

Conclusion:

Navigating the costs associated with RV travel requires a comprehensive approach that encompasses various aspects of ownership and exploration. From fuel and campground fees to maintenance and unexpected repairs, understanding the financial landscape of RV travel is crucial for effective budgeting. By carefully planning and considering all relevant expenses, you can embark on your RV adventure with confidence, knowing that you have a clear understanding of the financial commitments associated with this unique and rewarding lifestyle.

Money-Saving Tips

RV adventure doesn't have to break the bank. With thoughtful planning and strategic decisions, budget-conscious travelers can make the most of their journey while keeping costs in check. Here are some money-saving tips for those looking to explore the open road without overspending:

1. Fuel Efficiency Considerations:

Optimize fuel efficiency by maintaining a steady speed and avoiding sudden accelerations and decelerations. Plan routes that minimize detours and use fuel-efficient driving techniques. Additionally, consider using apps or websites that track fuel prices along your route, allowing you to fill up at the most cost-effective gas stations.

2. Campground Choices:

Campground fees can vary widely, so choose your campsites strategically. Public campgrounds, state parks, and national forests often offer more affordable options with beautiful natural surroundings. Consider boondocking, where camping is free on public lands, but be equipped with necessary amenities like solar power and waste disposal solutions.

3. Off-Peak Travel:

Traveling during off-peak seasons can lead to significant cost savings. Campground fees may be lower, attractions may offer discounted rates, and you'll likely encounter fewer crowds. Additionally, weekdays are generally less expensive than weekends for campground stays.

4. Discount Programs and Memberships:

Take advantage of discount programs and memberships designed for RV travelers. Joining clubs like Good Sam, Passport America, or Escapees can provide access to campground discounts, fuel savings, and other perks. These memberships often pay for themselves through the savings they offer.

5. Cooking in the RV:

Save on dining expenses by cooking your meals in the RV. Plan your meals, shop for groceries strategically, and take advantage of local produce and markets. Cooking in your RV not only saves money but also allows you to enjoy home-cooked meals on the road.

6. Technology for Savings:

Leverage technology to find the best deals. Use apps and websites to locate affordable campgrounds, compare fuel prices, and discover discounts on attractions. Technology can also help you plan efficient routes to minimize travel time and fuel costs.

7. Maintenance and DIY Repairs:

Regular maintenance is essential for RV longevity, but DIY skills can save money. Learn basic maintenance tasks like changing oil, checking tire pressure, and inspecting the RV's systems. By handling minor repairs yourself, you can avoid costly professional services.

8. Flexible Itinerary:

Embrace flexibility in your travel itinerary. Spontaneous decisions to stay at a more affordable campground or explore a less touristy area can lead to unexpected savings. Be open to adjusting your plans based on budget-friendly opportunities that arise during your journey.

9. Public Land Camping:

Take advantage of public lands for camping. Many Bureau of Land Management (BLM) areas and national forests allow free or low-cost camping. Research and plan your route to include stops at these budget-friendly locations.

10. Pack Light and Minimize:

Weight affects fuel efficiency, so pack only the essentials. Minimize the items you carry, and consider lightweight alternatives. This not only saves on fuel costs but also makes your RV more maneuverable and efficient.

11. Long-Term Stays:

Consider long-term stays at campgrounds or RV parks, as many offer discounted rates for extended periods. Monthly rates are often more economical than daily or weekly fees. This approach allows you to settle in, explore the surrounding area at a relaxed pace, and save money.

12. Free Entertainment:

Seek out free or low-cost entertainment options. Many cities and towns host events, festivals, or activities that are open to the public. Enjoy hiking, biking, or exploring nature, which often comes with no cost.

13. Reuse and Recycle:

Adopt a sustainable lifestyle by reusing and recycling items. Invest in reusable containers, water bottles, and utensils to reduce the need for disposable products. This not only saves money over time but also aligns with eco-friendly practices.

14. Community Sharing:

Engage with the RV community for shared resources. Some RV parks have community spaces with libraries, shared tools, and equipment. Collaborate with fellow RVers to swap items, tips, and even organize group activities that can lead to cost savings.

15. Budget Tracking:

Keep a detailed budget to track your expenses. Use apps or spreadsheets to monitor spending on fuel, campgrounds, groceries, and other categories. Regularly reviewing your budget helps identify areas where you can adjust spending and maximize savings.

In conclusion, savvy planning and conscious decision-making can significantly impact the affordability of your RV journey. By implementing these money-saving tips, you can strike a balance between exploration and budget consciousness, ensuring that your RV adventure is not only enriching but also financially sustainable. Whether you're a full-time RVer or embarking on a short-term road trip, these strategies empower you to make the most of your travel experience without compromising your budgetary goals.

Book 7: Traveling with Family

Family-Friendly Activities

Embarking on an RV adventure as a family opens the door to a world of shared experiences, bonding, and the creation of lasting memories. To make the journey even more enjoyable for all family members, incorporating family-friendly activities and games is key. Here are some suggestions for activities that cater to various age groups and ensure a fun-filled RV travel experience:

1. Campfire Stories and Songs:

Gather around the campfire, whether at a campground or a cozy outdoor spot, and take turns telling stories or singing songs. This classic activity not only fosters creativity but also provides an opportunity for family members to share their favorite tales.

2. Scavenger Hunts:

Plan scavenger hunts at different stops along your route. Create lists of items or landmarks to find, encouraging everyone to explore their surroundings. Scavenger hunts add an element of adventure and curiosity to each destination.

3. Nature Bingo:

Design bingo cards featuring items commonly found in nature, such as birds, trees, or insects. As you travel, mark off the items when spotted. This game promotes observation skills and an appreciation for the natural world.

4. Outdoor Movie Nights:

Set up an outdoor movie night under the stars. Many RVs are equipped with exterior entertainment systems, but even a portable projector and screen can transform your RV's exterior into a cozy movie theater. Bring blankets, popcorn, and enjoy a cinematic experience together.

5. Travel Journaling:

Encourage each family member to keep a travel journal. They can document daily adventures, sketch landscapes, or jot down interesting observations. This not only captures the essence of the journey but also serves as a creative outlet.

6. Family Cookbook Project:

Create a family cookbook during your RV travels. Assign cooking nights to each family member, allowing them to choose and prepare a recipe. Document the recipes, along with any modifications or special touches, in a shared cookbook. This project combines culinary exploration with family collaboration.

7. Board Games and Card Games:

Pack a selection of board games and card games suitable for various age groups. From classics like Monopoly and Uno to newer family-friendly games, these options provide entertainment during downtime and rainy days.

8. Geo-Caching Adventures:

Explore the world of geo-caching, a real-world treasure hunt using GPS coordinates. Create or find geo-cache locations along your route, and let family members take turns navigating to the hidden treasures. It adds an element of excitement and discovery to your travels.

9. DIY Craft Sessions:

Engage in do-it-yourself (DIY) craft sessions. Bring art supplies, such as colored pencils, markers, paper, and glue, and create personalized postcards, travel-themed drawings, or even nature-inspired crafts. This hands-on activity encourages creativity and expression.

10. Bike Rides and Nature Walks:

Pack bicycles and explore the surroundings through bike rides or nature walks. Many RV parks and campgrounds offer trails suitable for family adventures. It's an active and healthy way to enjoy the outdoors together.

11. Communal Cooking Nights:

Designate nights for communal cooking, where family members collaborate on preparing a meal. Whether it's a barbecue, a campfire cookout, or a potluck-style dinner, shared cooking experiences strengthen family bonds.

12. Interactive Learning Games:

Incorporate educational games into your travels. Apps, trivia games, and geography challenges can turn the journey into a fun and interactive learning experience for kids and adults alike.

13. Family Photo Album Project:

Create a family photo album during your RV travels. Assign the role of the family photographer to different members, and compile the photos into an album. This visual chronicle captures the essence of each destination and serves as a cherished keepsake.

14. Star Gazing Nights:

On clear nights, engage in star gazing. Bring a telescope or simply lay out under the night sky, identifying constellations and sharing stories about the stars. This serene and awe-inspiring activity encourages appreciation for the vastness of the universe.

15. Team Building Challenges:

Organize team-building challenges that encourage cooperation and friendly competition. Whether it's setting up a tent, solving puzzles, or navigating an obstacle course, these challenges promote teamwork and laughter.

Incorporating these family-friendly activities into your RV travels not only adds excitement to the journey but also strengthens the bonds between family members. RV adventures provide a unique opportunity to share quality time, explore diverse landscapes, and create a treasure trove of shared memories. From outdoor games to creative projects, the road becomes a canvas for family fun and togetherness.

Education on the Road

For families choosing the nomadic lifestyle of RV travel, the question of education becomes a central consideration. Whether on a short-term road trip or adopting a full-time RV lifestyle, families with children have various educational options to ensure a well-rounded and enriching learning experience.

1. Homeschooling:

Homeschooling is a popular choice for RV-traveling families as it offers flexibility and customization. Parents can tailor the curriculum to their child's needs and interests, integrating real-world experiences into the learning process. Numerous online resources, textbooks, and educational materials cater to homeschooling, providing a structured approach to education while allowing families to adapt to their travel schedule.

2. Online Learning Platforms:

In the digital age, online learning platforms have become valuable resources for remote education. Families can explore platforms that offer comprehensive curricula, interactive lessons, and assessments. These platforms cover various subjects and grade levels, providing a well-rounded educational experience.

3. Remote Learning Programs:

Many traditional schools and educational institutions now offer remote learning programs. This option allows children to follow their school's curriculum while traveling with their families. Communication tools like video conferencing enable students to stay connected with teachers and classmates, ensuring a sense of continuity in their education.

4. Local Learning Experiences:

RV travel provides a unique opportunity for hands-on, experiential learning. Families can incorporate local experiences into their educational plan, visiting museums, historical sites, nature reserves, and cultural landmarks. These real-world encounters enrich the learning process, offering insights that go beyond traditional classroom settings.

5. State and National Park Programs:

Many state and national parks offer educational programs for children. Junior Ranger programs, guided nature walks, and educational workshops provide an immersive learning experience. Participating in these programs not only enhances academic knowledge but also fosters a love for nature and conservation.

6. Community and RV Park Resources:

RV parks and communities often organize educational activities for children. These may include science experiments, art classes, or group discussions. Engaging with other RV-traveling families can create a sense of community and shared learning experiences.

7. Educational Apps and Games:

Educational apps and games cater to various age groups and subjects, turning screen time into a valuable learning tool. From language learning apps to math games, these resources make education accessible on the go. Parents can integrate these apps into the daily routine for a blended learning approach.

8. Library Visits:

Visiting local libraries along the travel route allows families to access a wealth of educational resources. Libraries offer not only a diverse selection of books but also programs such as reading circles, storytelling sessions, and educational workshops. Library visits promote a love for reading and provide a quiet space for focused learning.

9. Cooperative Learning with Other Families:

Collaborating with other RV-traveling families creates a cooperative learning environment. Families can organize joint educational activities, share resources, and even create study groups. This approach fosters socialization and allows children to learn from their peers.

10. Field Trips and Educational Tours:

Plan educational field trips and tours to complement the curriculum. Whether exploring historical sites, science museums, or cultural institutions, these excursions provide hands-on learning experiences. Integrating field trips into the educational plan adds depth and context to academic subjects.

11. Journaling and Documentation:

Encourage children to maintain travel journals documenting their experiences, observations, and insights. Journaling not only hones writing skills but also serves as a record of their educational journey. Children can include drawings, photographs, and reflections in their journals, creating a personalized learning portfolio.

12. Local Cultural Immersion:

Immerse children in local cultures and communities. Learning about different cultures, traditions, and lifestyles broadens their perspectives and enhances their understanding of the world. Engaging with locals, attending cultural events, and trying regional cuisine contribute to a holistic education.

13. Educational Workbooks and Worksheets:

Educational workbooks and worksheets provide structured learning materials. Parents can choose resources aligned with their child's grade level and academic goals. These materials offer a balance of practice exercises, quizzes, and engaging activities to reinforce concepts.

14. Parent-Teacher Collaboration:

In the homeschooling context, the collaboration between parents and teachers plays a crucial role. Regular communication with teachers, whether through virtual meetings or email correspondence, ensures that children stay on track with their academic goals. This partnership fosters a supportive educational environment.

15. Life Skills and Practical Learning:

RV living inherently involves practical learning experiences. Children can actively participate in tasks like trip planning, budgeting, and navigation. These life skills contribute to their overall education, preparing them for independent and responsible adulthood.

In conclusion, education on the road for RV-traveling families is a dynamic and adaptable journey. The multitude of options, from homeschooling to online platforms and community collaborations, allows families to craft a personalized and enriching educational experience. The RV lifestyle becomes a classroom without borders, where exploration, discovery, and learning seamlessly intertwine to create a foundation for lifelong curiosity and growth.

Book 8: Working and RVing

Remote Work

(Photo of Kampus Production www.pexels.com)

The rise of remote work has revolutionized the way people approach their professional lives, allowing individuals to break free from traditional office spaces and embrace a lifestyle of location independence. For those embarking on RV travel, remote work becomes not just a possibility but a powerful means of sustaining the journey. Here's a comprehensive look at the options and considerations for remote work while on the road.

1. Digital Nomad Opportunities:

The term "digital nomad" aptly describes individuals who leverage technology to work remotely while traveling. Many professions, including writers, graphic designers, programmers, and marketing professionals, can seamlessly transition into digital nomadism. With a reliable internet connection, these professionals can perform their tasks from the comfort of their RV.

2. Freelancing Platforms:

Freelancing platforms like Upwork, Fiverr, and Freelancer offer a plethora of opportunities for remote work. RV travelers can create profiles showcasing their skills and expertise, attracting clients from around the world. Whether it's writing, graphic design, web development, or virtual assistance, freelancing platforms provide a diverse range of job options.

3. Remote Jobs and Job Boards:

Job boards dedicated to remote work, such as Remote OK, FlexJobs, and We Work Remotely, list job opportunities specifically tailored for remote professionals. RV travelers can explore these platforms to find remote positions across various industries, including customer service, project management, and software development.

4. Telecommuting with Existing Employers:

For individuals already employed, negotiating a remote work arrangement with their existing employers can be a viable option. Many companies, especially in the wake of the global shift to remote work, are open to flexible arrangements. Clear communication and demonstrating the feasibility of remote work can pave the way for this transition.

5. Online Teaching and Tutoring:

Education professionals can explore opportunities in online teaching and tutoring. Platforms like VIPKid and Chegg Tutors connect educators with students globally. Teaching languages, providing academic support, or offering specialized expertise can be fulfilling ways to earn income while on the road.

6. Affiliate Marketing and Blogging:

Creating a blog or engaging in affiliate marketing allows individuals to monetize their passions. Whether it's travel writing, product reviews, or niche expertise, generating income through affiliate partnerships and ad revenue can sustain the RV lifestyle. Consistency and building an audience are key to success in this realm.

7. Virtual Assistance Services:

The demand for virtual assistants continues to grow, offering a wide array of administrative services to businesses and entrepreneurs. Tasks may include email management, scheduling, data entry, and customer support. RV travelers with organizational and communication skills can find opportunities in this field.

8. Content Creation and YouTube:

Content creators can leverage platforms like YouTube to generate income through ad revenue, sponsorships, and affiliate marketing. Whether it's travel vlogs, educational content, or entertainment, building a YouTube channel can be a rewarding endeavor for RV travelers with a knack for storytelling and video production.

9. E-commerce and Dropshipping:

Launching an e-commerce business, particularly through dropshipping, allows entrepreneurs to sell products without the need for physical inventory. With the right product selection and marketing strategy, individuals can manage their online stores while traveling in their RVs.

10. Remote Consultancy and Coaching:

Professionals with expertise in specific fields can offer consultancy or coaching services remotely. Whether it's business consulting, career coaching, or personal development, providing valuable insights and guidance can be monetized through one-on-one sessions or group workshops.

11. Remote Coding and Development:

Software developers, programmers, and IT professionals can find remote opportunities in coding and development. Platforms like GitHub and Stack Overflow connect developers with projects, and companies often hire remote tech talent for various roles.

12. Social Media Management:

The demand for social media managers continues to rise as businesses recognize the importance of a strong online presence. RV travelers with social media expertise can offer management services to clients, creating content, scheduling posts, and engaging with audiences.

13. Remote Sales and Marketing:

Sales and marketing professionals can explore remote opportunities in lead generation, sales outreach, and digital marketing. Platforms like LinkedIn and email marketing tools enable individuals to connect with potential clients and customers remotely.

14. Photography and Stock Images:

RV travelers with photography skills can monetize their art by selling stock images. Platforms like Shutterstock, Adobe Stock, and iStock allow photographers to upload and sell their photos, providing a passive income stream.

15. RV-Specific Jobs:

Some job opportunities cater specifically to the RV community. RV park hosting, campground management, and workamping (combining work with camping) are examples of roles designed for individuals traveling in their RVs. These jobs often provide a combination of compensation and campsite accommodation.

Considerations and Tips:

While remote work offers flexibility, it's essential to consider factors such as internet connectivity, time zone differences, and the nature of the work. Here are some tips for successful remote work on the road:

Internet Connectivity: Prioritize locations with reliable internet access. Invest in mobile hotspots or signal boosters to enhance connectivity.

Time Management: Establish a routine that balances work responsibilities with exploration. Set clear boundaries to ensure a healthy work-life balance.

Communication Skills: Effective communication is crucial in remote work. Keep open lines of communication with clients, colleagues, or employers.

Planning and Organization: Plan your travel itinerary to align with work commitments. Stay organized with task management tools and calendars.

Networking: Engage in online communities, networking events, and industry groups to connect with fellow remote professionals.

Backup Plans: Have contingency plans for unexpected challenges, such as power outages or internet disruptions.

Remote work on the road not only sustains the RV lifestyle but also unlocks a world of possibilities for individuals seeking professional fulfillment and personal freedom. As technology continues to evolve, the road becomes a workplace, offering a dynamic blend of work and adventure for those who choose to embrace the digital nomad lifestyle.

Connectivity Solutions

In the age of digital nomadism and RV adventures, staying connected while on the road has become essential for both work and leisure. Whether you're a remote worker, a family on a road trip, or an enthusiast exploring new horizons, reliable connectivity enhances the RV experience. Here's a comprehensive guide to connectivity solutions to keep you online and engaged during your travels.

1. Mobile Hotspots:

Invest in a reliable mobile hotspot device. These portable devices use cellular networks to create a Wi-Fi network, allowing you to connect multiple devices. Choose a hotspot from a reputable provider with good coverage in the areas you plan to travel.

2. Cellular Signal Boosters:

Enhance your cellular signal strength with a signal booster. These devices amplify weak signals, potentially turning areas with poor reception into viable connectivity zones. Ensure compatibility with your carrier and RV size for optimal performance.

3. RV Park Wi-Fi:

Many RV parks and campgrounds offer Wi-Fi access. While convenient, the quality of RV park Wi-Fi can vary. Consider it a supplementary option and be prepared with alternative connectivity solutions for more reliable internet access.

4. Satellite Internet:

Satellite internet provides connectivity in remote areas where traditional cellular networks may be unavailable. Portable satellite dishes or roof-mounted antennas can be installed on your RV, offering a reliable connection even in off-the-grid locations.

5. Roaming Plans and SIM Cards:

Research international roaming plans offered by your mobile carrier if you plan to travel across borders. Alternatively, consider purchasing local SIM cards in each country for cost-effective data plans.

6. Antenna Upgrades:

Upgrade your RV's antennas for better signal reception. High-gain antennas for both cellular and Wi-Fi signals can significantly improve connectivity. Consider professional installation for optimal results.

7. Wi-Fi Extenders:

Wi-Fi extenders amplify existing Wi-Fi signals, making them useful when you're parked near a source of public or campground Wi-Fi. Choose a high-quality extender with good range to ensure a strong and stable connection.

8. Multi-Carrier Devices:

Some mobile hotspots and routers support multiple carriers, allowing you to switch between networks for the best available signal. This flexibility is particularly useful in areas with varying cellular coverage.

9. Public Wi-Fi Safety:

When using public Wi-Fi, prioritize security. Use virtual private networks (VPNs) to encrypt your internet connection, protecting your data from potential security threats on open networks.

10. Data Management Apps:

Monitor and manage your data usage with specialized apps. These apps help you track your data consumption, set usage limits, and receive alerts when approaching your data cap.

11. Work with Offline Apps:

Maximize offline capabilities by using apps that allow you to work or enjoy content without a constant internet connection. Download maps, documents, and entertainment in advance to access them offline.

12. MIMO Technology:

Multiple Input, Multiple Output (MIMO) technology in routers and hotspots improves data transfer speeds and reliability. Devices equipped with MIMO have multiple antennas to enhance signal reception and transmission.

13. In-Motion Satellite Systems:

For those who need continuous connectivity while the RV is in motion, consider in-motion satellite systems. These roof-mounted systems automatically track satellites, providing a stable internet connection while on the road.

14. Community Forums and Apps:

Stay informed about connectivity options and share experiences with fellow RV travelers through online forums and apps. Platforms like RVillage and iRV2 provide valuable insights into connectivity solutions, coverage maps, and user experiences.

15. Test and Plan Ahead:

Before hitting the road, test your connectivity solutions in different scenarios. Check signal strength in various locations, evaluate data speeds, and identify dead zones. Plan your route with connectivity in mind, selecting campgrounds and stops with reliable internet access.

Considerations and Tips:

Connectivity needs may vary based on your travel style, work requirements, and the number of devices used. Here are some additional considerations and tips:

Data Plans: Choose data plans that align with your usage patterns. Consider plans with higher data caps or unlimited options if you rely heavily on internet connectivity.

Network Compatibility: Ensure your devices are compatible with the networks available in the regions you plan to travel. Check coverage maps provided by carriers for insights into network availability.

Security Measures: Prioritize security by using strong passwords, enabling two-factor authentication, and keeping your devices and software updated. Regularly check for firmware updates for your connectivity devices.

Backup Solutions: Have backup solutions in place in case your primary connectivity option fails. This could include a combination of mobile hotspots, satellite internet, and public Wi-Fi.

Weather Considerations: Satellite internet may be affected by adverse weather conditions. Be aware of weather patterns and have alternative connectivity options during inclement weather.

In conclusion, the key to a successful and enjoyable RV journey lies in effective connectivity management. By combining multiple solutions, staying informed about technological advancements, and planning ahead, RV travelers can ensure a reliable and consistent internet connection wherever the road takes them. Staying connected enhances the overall travel experience, allowing you to work, stay entertained, and stay in touch with loved ones while exploring the wonders of the open road.

Book 9: Exploring National Parks and Landmarks

Highlighting Key Destinations

Commencing on an RV journey across the vast and diverse landscapes of the United States is a pilgrimage through a tapestry of natural wonders, cultural treasures, and hidden gems. From towering peaks and verdant forests to bustling cities and serene coastlines, the USA beckons travelers to explore its iconic destinations. Let's unravel the charm of key destinations, featuring both renowned national parks and lesser-known hidden gems, that make the RV travel experience truly extraordinary.

1. Yellowstone National Park (Wyoming, Montana, Idaho):

Widely regarded as the world's first national park, Yellowstone is a geological marvel with its geysers, hot springs, and diverse wildlife. Old Faithful, Mammoth Hot Springs, and the Grand Canyon of the Yellowstone are must-visit landmarks. RV travelers can enjoy a mix of camping options, from developed campgrounds to backcountry sites.

2. Grand Canyon National Park (Arizona):

The Grand Canyon, a testament to the forces of nature, is a staggering display of layered rock formations carved by the Colorado River. RV enthusiasts can explore the South Rim, home to iconic viewpoints like Mather Point and Yavapai Observation Station. For a more secluded experience, the North Rim offers a quieter atmosphere and breathtaking vistas.

3. Yosemite National Park (California):

Yosemite's granite cliffs, waterfalls, and giant sequoias make it a haven for nature lovers. El Capitan and Half Dome are iconic rock formations, while Yosemite Valley boasts scenic wonders. RV-friendly campgrounds like Upper Pines and Wawona make it convenient for travelers to immerse themselves in the park's beauty.

4. Great Smoky Mountains National Park (North Carolina, Tennessee):

Straddling the border between North Carolina and Tennessee, the Great Smoky Mountains National Park is renowned for its mist-covered peaks, vibrant forests, and diverse wildlife. Cades Cove, Clingmans Dome, and Roaring Fork Motor Nature Trail are highlights that showcase the park's natural splendor.

5. Zion National Park (Utah):

Zion captivates visitors with its towering sandstone cliffs, slot canyons, and the meandering Virgin River. The Narrows and Angels Landing are iconic hikes, providing stunning views of the park's dramatic landscapes. RV travelers can stay at the South Campground, conveniently located near the park's shuttle system.

6. Acadia National Park (Maine):

On the rugged coast of Maine, Acadia National Park offers a captivating blend of rocky shorelines, dense forests, and Cadillac Mountain's summit views. The Park Loop Road provides easy access to scenic spots, while the Jordan Pond Path and Precipice Trail offer more challenging adventures for hikers.

7. Arches National Park (Utah):

A surreal landscape of more than 2,000 natural stone arches defines Arches National Park. Delicate Arch, Landscape Arch, and Balanced Rock are iconic formations that draw visitors seeking the park's unique geological features. RV travelers can explore the park's wonders via the scenic drive and numerous hiking trails.

8. Mount Rushmore National Memorial (South Dakota):

Mount Rushmore, a colossal sculpture featuring the faces of Presidents Washington, Jefferson, Roosevelt, and Lincoln, stands as a patriotic symbol. RV travelers can visit the memorial, attend the evening lighting ceremony, and explore nearby attractions like Crazy Horse Memorial and Custer State Park.

9. Sedona (Arizona):

Nestled amid striking red rock formations, Sedona is a hidden gem known for its spiritual energy and outdoor adventures. RV-friendly campgrounds like Rancho Sedona RV Park provide a tranquil base for exploring the area's hiking trails, vortex sites, and the artsy Tlaquepaque Village.

10. Outer Banks (North Carolina):

The Outer Banks, a string of barrier islands off the coast of North Carolina, boast pristine beaches, historic sites, and unique maritime culture. RV travelers can explore the Wright Brothers National Memorial, climb the Cape Hatteras Lighthouse, and enjoy beachside camping at Cape Point Campground.

11. Bryce Canyon National Park (Utah):

Bryce Canyon's intricate hoodoos and amphitheaters create a mesmerizing landscape. Sunrise Point, Sunset Point, and Bryce Point offer breathtaking views. RV campers can stay at the Bryce Canyon Pines RV Park, conveniently located near the park entrance.

12. Glacier National Park (Montana):

Known as the "Crown of the Continent," Glacier National Park enchants visitors with its rugged mountains, alpine lakes, and glaciers. Going-to-the-Sun Road provides access to stunning vistas, while Many Glacier and Two Medicine are popular areas for hiking and wildlife viewing. RV-friendly campgrounds like Fish Creek and St. Mary offer convenient accommodations.

13. Havasu Falls (Arizona):

Tucked within the Grand Canyon, Havasu Falls is a hidden oasis renowned for its vibrant turquoise waters. Accessible via a challenging hike or helicopter ride, Havasu Falls offers RV travelers a unique and rewarding adventure in the heart of the desert.

14. Cape Cod (Massachusetts):

Cape Cod's charming villages, lighthouses, and pristine beaches make it a beloved destination. RV-friendly campgrounds like Nickerson State Park and Shady Knoll Campground provide a comfortable base for exploring the Cape's maritime beauty and historic sites.

15. Big Sur (California):

Stretching along the rugged California coastline, Big Sur captivates with its dramatic cliffs, redwood forests, and panoramic ocean views. RV travelers can traverse the iconic Pacific Coast Highway, stopping at McWay Falls, Bixby Creek Bridge, and Pfeiffer Big Sur State Park for a quintessential Big Sur experience.

16. Shenandoah National Park (Virginia):

The Blue Ridge Mountains come alive in Shenandoah National Park, offering stunning vistas along the Skyline Drive. RV travelers can embark on scenic hikes, explore waterfalls, and experience the park's diverse flora and fauna. Campgrounds like Big Meadows and Loft Mountain provide convenient accommodations.

17. Olympic National Park (Washington):

Olympic National Park encompasses diverse ecosystems, from lush rainforests and alpine peaks to rugged coastline. RV enthusiasts can drive the scenic Hurricane Ridge Road, hike to Sol Duc Falls, and explore the enchanting Hoh Rainforest. RV-friendly campgrounds like Kalaloch and Sol Duc Hot Springs offer a gateway to the park's wonders.

18. Monument Valley (Arizona, Utah):

Monument Valley, with its iconic red sandstone buttes and mesas, is a symbol of the American West. RV travelers can take a guided tour through the valley's iconic landmarks, including the Mittens and Merrick Butte. Campgrounds in the surrounding area provide a unique opportunity to experience the vast desert landscape.

19. Joshua Tree National Park (California):

Joshua Tree National Park, where the Mojave and Colorado Deserts meet, is known for its otherworldly landscapes and distinctive Joshua Trees. RV visitors can explore the Skull Rock trail, stargaze in the clear desert night skies, and enjoy the unique rock formations. Campgrounds like Jumbo Rocks and Belle Campground cater to RV travelers.

20. Alaska's Kenai Peninsula (Alaska):

The Kenai Peninsula in Alaska offers a wilderness paradise with fjords, glaciers, and wildlife. RV travelers can cruise the Kenai Fjords, hike to Exit Glacier, and enjoy world-class fishing in the region. RV parks like Diamond M Ranch Resort provide a comfortable base for exploring this remote and stunning landscape.

21. Lassen Volcanic National Park (California):

Lassen Volcanic National Park showcases an array of geothermal wonders, including boiling springs and bubbling mud pots. RV visitors can drive the Lassen Volcanic National Park Highway, hike to Bumpass Hell, and witness the park's hydrothermal features. Manzanita Lake Campground and Summit Lake North Campground accommodate RV travelers.

22. Canyonlands National Park (Utah):

Canyonlands National Park, carved by the Colorado River, features mesmerizing canyons, arches, and buttes. RV travelers can explore the Island in the Sky and Needles districts, hike to Mesa Arch, and take in the panoramic views from Grand View Point. RV-friendly campgrounds like Willow Flat and Squaw Flat provide convenient access to the park's wonders.

23. The Florida Keys (Florida):

The string of tropical islands known as the Florida Keys offers a laid-back atmosphere, coral reefs, and vibrant marine life. RV enthusiasts can drive the Overseas Highway, explore Key West's historic streets, and indulge in water activities. RV parks like Boyd's Key West Campground provide a waterfront haven for travelers.

24. Devils Tower National Monument (Wyoming):

Rising dramatically from the Wyoming landscape, Devils Tower is a sacred site and geological wonder. RV travelers can witness the tower's majesty, hike the Tower Trail, and enjoy panoramic views from Joyner Ridge. Campgrounds in the area offer a tranquil setting for exploring this iconic landmark.

25. Cumberland Island National Seashore (Georgia):

Cumberland Island, off the coast of Georgia, is a pristine barrier island known for its wild horses, historic ruins, and unspoiled beaches. RV travelers can take a ferry to the island, explore Dungeness Ruins, and enjoy the serenity of the natural surroundings. Campgrounds near the ferry departure point provide convenient access to this coastal gem.

26. Cape Flattery (Washington):

The northwesternmost point of the contiguous United States, Cape Flattery offers breathtaking views of sea stacks, cliffs, and the Pacific Ocean. RV travelers can hike the Cape Flattery Trail, exploring the rugged beauty of the Olympic Peninsula. Nearby RV parks provide a peaceful retreat after a day of exploration.

27. Black Hills and Badlands (South Dakota):

The Black Hills and Badlands region in South Dakota beckons with its unique landscapes, including rugged canyons and the iconic Mount Rushmore. RV travelers can explore Custer State Park, visit Wind Cave National Park, and experience the scenic drives of the Needles Highway. RV campgrounds in the area provide a comfortable base for discovering this diverse region.

28. Great Sand Dunes National Park and Preserve (Colorado):

Home to the tallest sand dunes in North America, Great Sand Dunes National Park offers a surreal landscape of towering dunes and sweeping views. RV visitors can hike to the High Dune, sandboard down the slopes, and stargaze in the clear night skies. Pinon Flats Campground provides RV-friendly accommodations near the park entrance.

29. New Orleans (Louisiana):

Immerse yourself in the vibrant culture of New Orleans, known for its jazz music, historic architecture, and lively festivals. RV travelers can explore the French Quarter, indulge in Creole cuisine, and experience the city's unique charm. RV parks like French Quarter RV Resort offer a convenient location for discovering the lively spirit of the Big Easy.

30. Lighthouses of the Outer Banks (North Carolina):

The Outer Banks of North Carolina are dotted with historic lighthouses, each with its own maritime tale. RV enthusiasts can visit the Cape Hatteras Lighthouse, climb the Bodie Island Lighthouse, and explore the Roanoke Marshes Light. RV campgrounds along the Outer Banks provide a scenic and coastal setting for a memorable journey.

31. Joshua Tree Music Festival (California):

For music enthusiasts exploring Joshua Tree National Park, the Joshua Tree Music Festival offers a unique blend of live performances amid the desert landscape. RV travelers can camp at designated festival sites, enjoying a harmonious fusion of nature and music under the starry skies.

32. Chaco Culture National Historical Park (New Mexico):

Delve into the rich history of the ancestral Puebloan people at Chaco Culture National Historical Park. RV visitors can explore ancient ruins, such as Pueblo Bonito and Chetro Ketl, gaining insights into the cultural and architectural achievements of this UNESCO World Heritage Site.

33. Apostle Islands National Lakeshore (Wisconsin):

The Apostle Islands, nestled in Lake Superior, boast sea caves, lighthouses, and pristine shorelines. RV travelers can take a ferry to explore the islands, kayak through sea caves, and witness the captivating sea stacks. RV parks along the Lake Superior coastline provide a picturesque backdrop for this maritime adventure.

34. Taos Pueblo (New Mexico):

Immerse yourself in Native American history and culture at Taos Pueblo, a UNESCO World Heritage Site. RV visitors can tour the ancient adobe structures, witness traditional ceremonies, and explore the vibrant arts and crafts of the Taos community.

35. Natchez Trace Parkway (Mississippi, Alabama, Tennessee):

Follow the historic Natchez Trace Parkway, a scenic route that winds through lush forests, historic sites, and Native American burial mounds. RV travelers can experience the tranquility of the parkway, discovering landmarks like the Emerald Mound and Mount Locust, while enjoying RV-friendly campsites along the way.

36. Antelope Canyon (Arizona):

Antelope Canyon, with its mesmerizing slot canyons, showcases the artistry of wind and water sculpting the Navajo sandstone. RV enthusiasts can join guided tours to explore Upper and Lower Antelope Canyon, capturing the play of light and shadow in these natural wonders.

37. Mammoth Cave National Park (Kentucky):

Uncover the subterranean wonders of Mammoth Cave, the world's longest known cave system. RV travelers can take guided cave tours, marveling at intricate formations and underground chambers. RV campgrounds near the park provide convenient access to this geological marvel.

38. The Berkshires (Massachusetts):

The Berkshires, a picturesque region in western Massachusetts, offer a blend of cultural attractions, scenic landscapes, and outdoor recreation. RV travelers can explore cultural hubs like Tanglewood, hike the Appalachian Trail, and enjoy the vibrant arts scene in towns like Lenox and Stockbridge.

39. Bonneville Salt Flats (Utah):

The vast expanse of the Bonneville Salt Flats is a surreal landscape where the horizon seems to stretch endlessly. RV visitors can experience the unique terrain, especially during events like the Speed Week, where land-speed records are attempted on the salt flats.

40. Luray Caverns (Virginia):

Descend into the mesmerizing underground world of Luray Caverns, an intricate cave system adorned with stalactites and stalagmites. RV travelers can tour the caverns, marveling at formations like the Great Stalacpipe Organ, creating a symphony of sounds within the cavern's chambers.

41. Lake Tahoe (California, Nevada):

Nestled in the Sierra Nevada, Lake Tahoe is a pristine alpine lake surrounded by snow-capped peaks. RV enthusiasts can explore the lake's shores, indulge in water activities, and enjoy panoramic views from Emerald Bay State Park. RV parks along the lake offer a serene retreat in this mountainous paradise.

42. Petrified Forest National Park (Arizona):

Witness the remnants of an ancient forest turned to stone at Petrified Forest National Park. RV travelers can drive through the park's Painted Desert, marvel at petrified logs, and explore archaeological sites like Puerco Pueblo. RV-friendly campgrounds provide an opportunity to delve into the park's geological wonders.

43. Charleston (South Carolina):

Charleston, steeped in history and Southern charm, invites RV travelers to stroll through cobblestone streets, explore antebellum architecture, and savor Lowcountry cuisine. RV parks near Charleston provide a convenient base for discovering the city's historic districts, plantations, and waterfront delights.

44. Blue Ridge Parkway (Virginia, North Carolina):

The Blue Ridge Parkway, often referred to as "America's Favorite Drive," winds through the Appalachian Highlands, offering breathtaking views of rolling mountains and valleys. RV travelers can experience the parkway's scenic overlooks, hiking trails, and cultural exhibits, creating a memorable journey through the heart of the Blue Ridge Mountains.

45. Carlsbad Caverns National Park (New Mexico):

Venture into the vast underground chambers of Carlsbad Caverns, a geological marvel filled with stalactites, stalagmites, and intricate formations. RV visitors can explore the caverns via guided tours or the self-guided Natural Entrance route. RV-friendly campgrounds near the park provide a comfortable haven for travelers to recharge after a day of exploration.

46. The Everglades (Florida):

The Everglades, a unique ecosystem of wetlands and mangroves, is a haven for wildlife enthusiasts. RV travelers can explore the Anhinga Trail, take an airboat tour through the sawgrass prairies, and spot alligators and diverse bird species. RV parks in the surrounding area offer a gateway to this expansive wilderness.

47. San Juan Islands (Washington):

The San Juan Islands, nestled in the Salish Sea, beckon RV travelers with their scenic beauty and abundant marine life. Ferries connect RV enthusiasts to islands like Orcas, Lopez, and San Juan, where they can explore charming villages, whale watch, and enjoy the tranquility of island life.

48. Great Basin National Park (Nevada):

Great Basin National Park, known for its dark skies and ancient bristlecone pine trees, provides a serene escape. RV visitors can hike the Wheeler Peak Trail, explore the Lehman Caves, and stargaze at the park's designated Dark Sky site. RV-friendly campgrounds offer a peaceful retreat in this high-altitude sanctuary.

49. Big Bend National Park (Texas):

Big Bend National Park, nestled along the Rio Grande, offers a rugged landscape of canyons, desert, and riverfront. RV travelers can explore the Chisos Mountains, float along the Rio Grande, and experience the park's diverse ecosystems. RV campgrounds like Rio Grande Village provide a convenient base for immersing in the park's natural wonders.

50. Monument Valley Navajo Tribal Park (Arizona, Utah):

Monument Valley, managed by the Navajo Nation, boasts iconic sandstone buttes and mesas that have served as the backdrop for countless Western films. RV enthusiasts can take guided tours led by Navajo guides, exploring the valley's stunning formations and learning about the cultural significance of this sacred land.

51. Mackinac Island (Michigan):

Transport yourself to a bygone era on Mackinac Island, where horse-drawn carriages replace automobiles, and Victorian architecture lines the streets. RV travelers can take a ferry to the island, explore historic sites like Fort Mackinac, and savor the charm of this car-free destination.

52. Cappadocia of the Ozarks - Eureka Springs (Arkansas):

Eureka Springs, often referred to as the "Cappadocia of the Ozarks," captivates with its unique architecture, winding streets, and eclectic arts scene. RV visitors can explore historic downtown, tour the Thorncrown Chapel, and indulge in the town's vibrant arts and culture. RV parks in the area provide a scenic retreat near this Ozark gem.

53. Redwood National and State Parks (California):

The towering redwoods of Northern California stand as sentinels in Redwood National and State Parks. RV travelers can drive the Avenue of the Giants, hike among the ancient trees, and marvel at giants like the Hyperion, the world's tallest known living tree. RV-friendly campgrounds offer an immersive experience in the land of giants.

54. Apostle Islands Ice Caves (Wisconsin):

During the winter months, the Apostle Islands transform into a winter wonderland, adorned with ice formations and frozen caves along the Lake Superior shoreline. Brave RV travelers can experience this icy spectacle, exploring the ice caves and marveling at the beauty of winter on the Great Lakes.

55. San Francisco (California):

San Francisco, a city renowned for its iconic landmarks and progressive culture, invites RV travelers to explore the Golden Gate Bridge, visit Alcatraz Island, and meander through neighborhoods like Chinatown and Haight-Ashbury. RV parks in the Bay Area provide a convenient base for discovering the eclectic charm of the City by the Bay.

56. Gulf Shores and Orange Beach (Alabama):

The Gulf Shores and Orange Beach offer pristine white-sand beaches, warm Gulf waters, and a laid-back coastal atmosphere. RV enthusiasts can relax on the beaches, explore Bon Secour National Wildlife Refuge, and enjoy fresh seafood. RV parks along the Gulf Coast provide a sunny retreat for those seeking a coastal getaway.

57. Olympic Peninsula Loop (Washington):

The Olympic Peninsula Loop takes RV travelers on a scenic journey around the diverse landscapes of the peninsula, from the lush rainforests of the Hoh to the rugged coastline of Rialto Beach. RV-friendly campsites provide opportunities to explore Olympic National Park, visit lavender farms, and witness the beauty of the Pacific Northwest.

58. Napa Valley (California):

Napa Valley, renowned for its vineyards and wineries, beckons RV travelers to indulge in wine tasting, scenic drives, and culinary delights. RV parks in the region offer a relaxing base for exploring the picturesque vineyard-covered hills and charming towns like Yountville and St. Helena.

59. Custer State Park (South Dakota):

Custer State Park, often referred to as the "crown jewel" of South Dakota, boasts scenic drives, granite peaks, and a diverse array of wildlife. RV enthusiasts can drive the Needles Highway, witness the annual buffalo roundup, and enjoy the serenity of Sylvan Lake. RV-friendly campgrounds provide a rustic retreat in the heart of the Black Hills.

60. Vicksburg National Military Park (Mississippi):

History comes alive at Vicksburg National Military Park, where RV travelers can explore Civil War battlefields, visit the USS Cairo Museum, and witness panoramic views from the Vicksburg National Cemetery. RV parks in the area provide a contemplative setting for reflecting on the historical significance of this landmark.

Planning Tips for RV Travelers:

To make the most of your RV journey to these iconic destinations and hidden gems, consider the following planning tips:

Reservations: For popular national parks and campgrounds, especially during peak seasons, consider making reservations in advance to secure your preferred campsite.

Seasonal Considerations: Be mindful of seasonal weather patterns when planning your visit. Some destinations, like Glacier National Park, have limited accessibility during winter months.

Route Planning: Create a flexible itinerary that allows for spontaneous detours and exploration. Utilize maps, GPS apps, and travel resources to plan the most scenic and RV-friendly routes.

RV-Friendly Accommodations: Research RV campgrounds and parks along your route. Look for amenities such as full hookups, dump stations, and proximity to key attractions.

National Park Pass: Consider purchasing a National Park Pass, which provides entry to multiple national parks and federal recreational lands, offering cost savings for avid RV travelers.

Check RV Regulations: Be aware of RV size restrictions and regulations in national parks and other destinations. Some parks may have limitations on vehicle length, so plan accordingly.

Guided Tours

RV journey across the United States opens up a world of diverse landscapes, historical sites, and cultural gems. As you traverse the open road, the opportunity to enhance your exploration with guided tours and activities at each destination adds a layer of depth and knowledge to your adventure. Here's a curated selection of recommended guided tours and activities to consider at some of the iconic destinations you might encounter on your RV trip:

1. Yellowstone National Park (Wyoming, Montana, Idaho):

Guided Wildlife Safari: Engage with the park's abundant wildlife, including grizzly bears, wolves, and bison, through a guided safari. Knowledgeable naturalists provide insights into the park's ecology and behavior of its iconic inhabitants.

Old Faithful Tour: Join a guided tour to witness the majestic Old Faithful geyser erupting in all its splendor. Learn about the geothermal features of the park and explore nearby geysers and hot springs.

2. Grand Canyon National Park (Arizona):

Helicopter Tour: Soar above the Grand Canyon's vast expanse on a helicopter tour, offering breathtaking views of the canyon's rugged terrain and the Colorado River winding through its depths.

Mule Ride to Phantom Ranch: Embark on a mule ride descending into the canyon, culminating at Phantom Ranch. Experienced guides lead the journey, sharing insights into the geological wonders of the Grand Canyon.

3. Yosemite National Park (California):

Guided Photography Hike: Explore Yosemite's scenic beauty with a professional photographer guide. Capture the park's iconic landmarks, including Half Dome and Yosemite Falls, while receiving photography tips and insights.

Stargazing Tour: Yosemite's dark skies provide an ideal canvas for stargazing. Join an astronomy tour to observe constellations, planets, and the Milky Way, guided by experts with telescopes.

4. Zion National Park (Utah):

Narrows Guided Hike: Venture into the renowned Narrows on a guided hike, wading through the Virgin River amidst towering canyon walls. Guides offer safety tips and share the geological history of this unique slot canyon.

Canyoneering Adventure: For thrill-seekers, join a canyoneering tour to explore the park's narrow slot canyons, rappelling down cliffs, and navigating through the stunning red rock landscapes.

5. Acadia National Park (Maine):

Guided Sea Kayaking: Experience the coastal beauty of Acadia by joining a guided sea kayaking tour. Paddle along the rugged shoreline, explore sea caves, and enjoy the serenity of the park from a unique perspective.

Sunrise Summit Tour: Ascend Cadillac Mountain to catch the first rays of the sun in the United States. A guided sunrise tour provides historical context and geological insights as you witness the spectacular dawn.

6. Arches National Park (Utah):

Fiery Furnace Guided Hike: Navigate the intricate sandstone fins of the Fiery Furnace with a knowledgeable guide. This off-the-beaten-path adventure offers insights into the park's unique geological formations.

Stargazing in the Desert: Join an evening stargazing tour in the desert surroundings of Arches. Away from light pollution, the night sky comes alive, and astronomers guide you through celestial wonders.

7. Mount Rushmore National Memorial (South Dakota):

Evening Lighting Ceremony: Attend the iconic evening lighting ceremony at Mount Rushmore, where the faces of the presidents are illuminated against the night sky. Park rangers provide historical context during this patriotic event.

Black Hills Gold Factory Tour: Discover the artistry behind Black Hills Gold jewelry with a guided tour of a local gold factory. Learn about the crafting process and the cultural significance of this unique jewelry.

8. Glacier National Park (Montana):

Red Bus Tour: Traverse the Going-to-the-Sun Road in style aboard a historic red bus. A guided tour provides narration about the park's history, wildlife, and the geological forces that shaped the landscape.

Boat Tour on Lake McDonald: Explore the pristine waters of Lake McDonald on a guided boat tour. Learn about the park's glacial history while enjoying the breathtaking mountain scenery.

9. Havasu Falls (Arizona):

Havasu Falls Guided Hike: Navigate the challenging trail to Havasu Falls with a knowledgeable guide. Learn about the Havasupai Tribe's cultural connection to the area and the geological formations that create the turquoise waters.

Cultural Experience with Havasupai Tribe: Engage in a guided cultural experience with members of the Havasupai Tribe. Gain insights into their traditions, storytelling, and the significance of the Havasu Falls area.

10. Outer Banks (North Carolina):

Wild Horse Safari: Explore the beaches of the Outer Banks in search of the wild Spanish Mustangs that roam freely. Guided safari tours provide a unique opportunity to witness these majestic horses in their natural habitat.

Wright Brothers National Memorial Tour: Visit the Wright Brothers National Memorial and join a guided tour to delve into the history of aviation. Explore the site where the Wright brothers achieved the first powered flight, and learn about their pioneering contributions to aviation.

11. Everglades National Park (Florida):

Airboat Tour: Glide through the wetlands and mangroves of the Everglades on an airboat tour. Knowledgeable guides provide insights into the park's unique ecosystem, and you may encounter alligators, manatees, and a variety of bird species.

Ranger-Led Swamp Walk: Join a ranger-led swamp walk to explore the park on foot. Gain a deeper understanding of the Everglades' flora and fauna while traversing boardwalks and trails with an experienced naturalist.

12. New Orleans (Louisiana):

French Quarter Walking Tour: Immerse yourself in the rich cultural tapestry of New Orleans with a guided walking tour of the French Quarter. Discover historic landmarks, hear stories of the city's past, and savor the vibrant atmosphere.

Steamboat Jazz Cruise: Embark on a steamboat jazz cruise along the Mississippi River. Enjoy live jazz music, indulge in Creole cuisine, and witness the city's skyline from the vantage point of the iconic river.

13. Charleston (South Carolina):

Historic Carriage Tour: Explore the charming streets of Charleston on a historic carriage tour. Led by knowledgeable guides and drawn by horses, these tours provide insights into the city's antebellum architecture and rich history.

Gullah Culture Experience: Engage in a guided Gullah culture experience to learn about the traditions and language of the Gullah people, descendants of African Americans who lived in the Lowcountry.

14. San Francisco (California):

Alcatraz Island Tour: Journey to Alcatraz Island for a guided tour of the infamous former prison. Learn about the history of "The Rock," the lives of its prisoners, and the captivating escape attempts.

Cable Car Museum Visit: Discover the history of San Francisco's iconic cable cars at the Cable Car Museum. Guided tours showcase the mechanisms and engineering behind these historic modes of transportation.

15. Key West (Florida):

Snorkeling Adventure: Delve into the vibrant marine life of Key West with a guided snorkeling adventure. Explore coral reefs, encounter tropical fish, and perhaps swim with friendly sea turtles under the guidance of experienced instructors.

Hemingway House Tour: Visit the former home of renowned author Ernest Hemingway on a guided tour. Learn about Hemingway's life in Key West, explore the lush gardens, and encounter the descendants of his famous six-toed cats.

16. Niagara Falls (New York):

Maid of the Mist Boat Tour: Experience the awe-inspiring power of Niagara Falls up close on a Maid of the Mist boat tour. Guided tours take you to the base of the falls, providing a thrilling and immersive perspective.

Cave of the Winds Tour: Join a guided Cave of the Winds tour to stand on wooden walkways at the base of Bridal Veil Falls. Feel the rush of the falls and witness the natural beauty of Niagara from a unique vantage point.

17. Zion National Park (Utah):

Angels Landing Guided Hike: Conquer the iconic Angels Landing trail with the assistance of a knowledgeable guide. This challenging hike offers stunning panoramic views of Zion Canyon, and guides ensure safety and provide historical context.

Canyon Overlook Sunset Tour: Opt for a guided Canyon Overlook tour during the sunset hours. Witness the park's sandstone formations bathed in warm hues while learning about the geological processes that shaped Zion.

18. Mammoth Cave National Park (Kentucky):

Wild Cave Tour: For adventurous spirits, embark on a wild cave tour led by experienced guides. Explore Mammoth Cave's underground chambers, crawl through passages, and learn about the geological formations in this expansive cave system.

Historical Tour: Join a historical tour to delve into the rich cultural history of Mammoth Cave. Guides share stories of early explorers, slaves who mined saltpeter, and the cave's role during the War of 1812.

19. Mount Rainier National Park (Washington):

Guided Snowshoe Walk: In the winter months, join a guided snowshoe walk through the snow-covered landscapes of Mount Rainier. Guides provide equipment and share insights into the park's winter ecology.

Sunrise Photography Tour: Capture the sunrise over Mount Rainier on a guided photography tour. Learn techniques for capturing the perfect shot while enjoying the breathtaking alpenglow on the mountain.

20. Charleston Tea Garden (South Carolina):

Tea Factory Tour: Take a guided tour of the Charleston Tea Garden, the only tea plantation in North America. Learn about the tea-making process, from cultivation to harvesting, and savor a tasting of freshly brewed teas.

Trolley Tour of Wadmalaw Island: Explore the scenic beauty of Wadmalaw Island on a guided trolley tour. Discover the island's history, Gullah culture, and lush landscapes, including stops at notable landmarks.

Conclusion:

Integrating guided tours and activities into your RV journey elevates the travel experience, providing in-depth insights, adventure, and a deeper connection to the destinations you explore. Whether it's uncovering the secrets of a national park, immersing yourself in the culture of a city, or embarking on thrilling outdoor adventures, these guided experiences enrich the tapestry of your RV adventure, creating lasting memories along the way.

Book 10: Culinary Adventures on the Road

RV Cooking Tips

Embarking on an RV journey not only offers the thrill of exploration but also the opportunity to indulge in delicious meals cooked right in the compact kitchen of your mobile home. RV cooking is a unique experience that requires creativity, efficiency, and a bit of planning. Here are some RV cooking tips and easy recipes to ensure your culinary adventures on the road are as enjoyable as the destinations you visit.

1. Meal Planning and Prepping:

Plan your meals in advance to streamline your grocery shopping and optimize storage space. Consider ingredients that can be used in multiple dishes to minimize waste. Prepping ingredients ahead of time, such as chopping vegetables or marinating proteins, can save time and make cooking in the RV more efficient.

2. Compact Kitchen Essentials:

RV kitchens are compact, so it's essential to have versatile cooking tools. Invest in stackable pots and pans, collapsible measuring cups, and nesting bowls to maximize storage. Portable appliances like a compact slow cooker, instant pot, or an electric skillet can be valuable additions to your RV kitchen arsenal.

3. One-Pot Wonders:

Opt for one-pot or one-pan meals to simplify cooking and minimize cleanup. Dishes like stir-fries, pasta with sauce, and casseroles allow you to combine ingredients and cook them together, saving time and resources.

4. Grilling on the Go:

Take advantage of outdoor grilling options. Many RVs come equipped with built-in grills or have space for portable grills. Grilling not only adds a delicious smoky flavor to your meals but also reduces the need for extensive indoor cooking.

5. Stocking Your RV Pantry:

Maintain a well-stocked pantry with essential ingredients like canned goods, pasta, rice, and a variety of spices. This ensures you have the basics on hand for creating diverse and flavorful meals without the need for frequent grocery stops.

6. Eco-Friendly Cooking:

Embrace eco-friendly cooking practices by using reusable containers, minimizing single-use items, and choosing fresh, local produce when available. Consider investing in silicone storage bags, bamboo utensils, and reusable containers to reduce your environmental footprint.

7. Easy and Quick RV Recipes:

RV Breakfast Burritos:

Ingredients: Eggs, tortillas, diced vegetables, cheese, and precooked sausage or bacon.

Instructions: Scramble eggs and cook with diced vegetables and pre-cooked meat. Fill tortillas with the mixture, add cheese, and roll into burritos. Wrap in foil and heat on a grill or stovetop.

Campfire Quesadillas:

Ingredients: Flour tortillas, shredded cheese, cooked chicken (canned or pre-cooked), and optional salsa.

Instructions: Place tortilla on a griddle or pan, add cheese, chicken, and salsa. Top with another tortilla. Cook until cheese is melted, flipping halfway through.

Instant Pot Chili:

Ingredients: Ground beef, beans, diced tomatoes, tomato sauce, chili seasoning, and optional toppings.

Instructions: Brown ground beef in the Instant Pot, add beans, diced tomatoes, tomato sauce, and chili seasoning. Cook on high pressure for a quick and flavorful chili.

8. Efficient Cleaning Tips:

Keep cleaning supplies organized in your RV. Use collapsible dishpans for washing dishes, and consider biodegradable and environmentally friendly cleaning products. Wipe down surfaces regularly to maintain a clean and efficient kitchen space.

9. Fresh and Local Ingredients:

Take advantage of local farmers' markets and grocery stores along your route. Fresh, local ingredients can elevate your meals, providing a taste of the regional flavors you encounter on your journey.

10. Community Cookbook Exchange:

Engage with the RV community by participating in a cookbook exchange. Share your favorite RV-friendly recipes with fellow travelers and discover new culinary inspirations from others on the road.

In conclusion, RV cooking is a delightful aspect of the nomadic lifestyle, offering a chance to experiment with flavors, make the most of limited kitchen space, and savor meals against the backdrop of diverse landscapes. By planning ahead, optimizing your kitchen setup, and embracing simple yet delicious recipes, you can turn your RV kitchen into a culinary haven on wheels. Whether you're grilling under the stars or whipping up a quick one-pot wonder, the joy of RV cooking lies in its simplicity and the shared experience of creating memorable meals on the open road.

Local Cuisine

RV journey across the United States not only exposes travelers to the country's breathtaking landscapes but also offers a delectable journey through diverse regional cuisines. From seafood on the coasts to barbecue in the South and hearty comfort food in the Midwest, the local flavors you encounter on your road trip add a savory dimension to your travel experience. Let's delve into the rich tapestry of regional dishes and where to find them along your nomadic journey.

1. New England:

Lobster Roll: In the northeastern coastal states, indulge in the iconic lobster roll. Fresh lobster meat, often mixed with mayo and herbs, is nestled in a buttered, toasted bun. Explore seafood shacks along the shores of Maine or Massachusetts for an authentic experience.

Clam Chowder: New England clam chowder, a creamy soup featuring tender clams, potatoes, onions, and bacon, is a comforting classic. Savor a bowl at waterfront restaurants or local diners throughout the region.

2. The South:

Barbecue: The South is synonymous with barbecue, and each state boasts its unique style. In Texas, relish beef brisket with a peppery rub, while in North Carolina, pulled pork with vinegar-based sauce takes center stage. Visit barbecue joints, roadside stands, or attend local festivals for a true taste of southern barbecue.

Shrimp and Grits: Head to the coastal areas of the Carolinas and Georgia for a taste of shrimp and grits. This dish combines succulent shrimp with creamy grits, often flavored with bacon, spices, and a rich sauce.

3. Midwest:

Deep-Dish Pizza (Chicago): Chicago is renowned for its deep-dish pizza. Enjoy a thick, hearty crust loaded with cheese, toppings, and chunky tomato sauce. Numerous pizzerias in the city serve this iconic dish.

Cheese Curds (Wisconsin): A Midwest road trip wouldn't be complete without sampling cheese curds in Wisconsin. These bite-sized nuggets of fresh cheese, often battered and deep-fried, are a local favorite at fairs, markets, and dairy farms.

4. Southwest:

Tex-Mex: In the Southwest, Tex-Mex cuisine takes center stage. Savor dishes like enchiladas, tacos, and tamales filled with a flavorful blend of spices, cheeses, and meats. Explore local Mexican restaurants or street vendors for an authentic taste.

Chile Rellenos (New Mexico): New Mexico is known for its chile rellenos, a dish featuring roasted and stuffed green chilies. Indulge in this flavorful and sometimes spicy delicacy at local eateries across the state.

5. Pacific Northwest:

Salmon and Seafood Chowder: In the Pacific Northwest, particularly in Washington and Oregon, fresh seafood is a culinary highlight. Enjoy succulent salmon prepared in various ways, from grilled to smoked. Dive into a comforting bowl of seafood chowder filled with clams, mussels, and tender fish.

Dungeness Crab (Oregon): Along the Oregon coast, savor Dungeness crab, a sweet and delicate treat. Seek out seafood markets or coastal restaurants for a taste of this Pacific Northwest specialty.

6. California:

Fish Tacos: California's coastal regions are synonymous with fresh and vibrant fish tacos. Grilled or battered fish, topped with slaw, salsa, and creamy sauces, make for a delightful beachside meal. Explore taco stands and seafood joints along the California coast.

Avocado Everything: California's love affair with avocados is evident in various dishes. From avocado toast for breakfast to guacamole with chips and avocado burgers for lunch, indulge in the state's avocado-centric creations.

7. Gulf Coast:

Gumbo (Louisiana): Head to Louisiana for a taste of gumbo, a rich and hearty stew featuring a mix of meats, seafood, and okra. Savor this soul-warming dish at local restaurants and eateries, especially in New Orleans.

Cajun and Creole Delights: Explore the Gulf Coast for a culinary journey through Cajun and Creole cuisines. Sample dishes like jambalaya, étouffée, and beignets in Louisiana and beyond.

8. Mid-Atlantic:

Cheesesteak (Philadelphia): A trip to Philadelphia calls for a classic cheesesteak experience. Thinly sliced beefsteak, melted cheese, and toppings like onions or peppers are stuffed into a roll. Visit local cheesesteak joints for an authentic Philly delight.

Blue Crab (Maryland): Maryland is famous for its blue crabs. Indulge in steamed crabs seasoned with Old Bay seasoning or enjoy crab cakes made with the region's prized blue crab meat.

As you traverse the diverse regions of the United States in your RV, embrace the opportunity to savor the unique and delicious local cuisines that define each area. From iconic dishes to hidden gems, the culinary journey is as integral to your adventure as the landscapes you explore. Explore local markets, diners, and eateries along your route, allowing your taste buds to savor the rich tapestry of flavors that make each region a gastronomic delight.

Book 11: Connecting with the RV Community

Socializing on the Road

Socializing on the road is a key aspect of the RV lifestyle, offering opportunities to connect with fellow enthusiasts, share experiences, and build a sense of community. The nomadic nature of RV travel doesn't mean you have to journey alone; in fact, it opens up avenues for meaningful interactions. Here are ways to foster connections with other RV enthusiasts:

1. RV Parks and Campgrounds:

RV parks and campgrounds serve as hubs for social interaction. Many of these places organize community events, potlucks, and group activities. Participate in organized events or simply strike up a conversation with your neighbors at the campsite. The shared love for RV life often serves as an instant conversation starter.

2. Online RV Communities:

Leverage the power of technology to connect with the RV community online. Numerous forums, social media groups, and websites cater to RV enthusiasts. Platforms like RVillage and iRV2 allow you to find and connect with like-minded travelers, share tips, and even plan meetups.

3. Attend RV Rallies and Gatherings:

RV rallies and gatherings are fantastic opportunities to meet a diverse array of RV enthusiasts. These events can be region-specific or themed, catering to various interests. From vintage RV rallies to full-timer meetups, attending these gatherings provides a chance to network and make lasting connections.

4. Join RV Clubs:

Many RV enthusiasts join clubs that align with their interests or demographics. Clubs like the Family Motor Coach Association (FMCA), Escapees, or Good Sam Club organize events, provide resources, and offer a sense of belonging within the larger RV community. Membership often includes access to exclusive gatherings and forums.

5. Volunteer Opportunities:

Engage in volunteer work at RV parks, campgrounds, or within local communities. Volunteering not only contributes positively to the places you visit but also provides a platform for meeting fellow travelers with a shared commitment to giving back.

6. Attend Workshops and Seminars:

Many RV parks and campgrounds host workshops and seminars on various topics, from maintenance tips to travel hacks. Participating in these educational events not only enhances your RV knowledge but also allows you to mingle with others who share your passion.

7. Collaborate on Travel Plans:

Share your travel plans with fellow RVers, and you might discover common routes or destinations. Collaborate on itineraries, convoy together, or plan meetups along the way. The shared journey can create bonds and turn fellow travelers into friends.

8. Create a Travel Blog or Vlog:

Documenting your RV adventures through a travel blog or vlog can attract a community of followers and fellow enthusiasts. Share your experiences, tips, and insights online, and engage with your audience. This can lead to connections with other travelers who resonate with your journey.

9. Use RV-Specific Apps:

Explore apps designed for RVers, such as RVillage, where you can connect with nearby RVers, join interest groups, and plan impromptu meetups. These apps facilitate real-time communication, making it easier to socialize on the go.

10. Attend Local Events:

Immerse yourself in local events and gatherings at the destinations you visit. Whether it's a farmers' market, a town festival, or a cultural celebration, these events provide opportunities to interact with locals and fellow travelers alike.

Socializing on the road as an RV enthusiast is about embracing the communal spirit of the lifestyle. Whether through in-person interactions at RV parks, online communities, or shared adventures on the open road, the RV community offers a unique and welcoming environment where connections can blossom. By actively seeking out opportunities to engage with others, you not only enhance your travel experience but also contribute to the vibrant tapestry of the RVing community.

RV Clubs and Gatherings

RV clubs and gatherings play a pivotal role in fostering a sense of community among enthusiasts, providing valuable support, resources, and opportunities for shared experiences. These clubs and events cater to a diverse range of interests, from specific types of RVs to lifestyle preferences. Here's a glimpse into the world of RV clubs and gatherings that contribute to the rich tapestry of the RV community:

1. Family Motor Coach Association (FMCA):

FMCA is one of the largest RV clubs, bringing together motorhome enthusiasts. It offers a plethora of benefits, including exclusive member discounts, educational resources, and a sense of camaraderie. FMCA organizes international and regional rallies, providing a platform for members to connect and share their passion for RVing.

2. Escapees RV Club:

Known for its focus on full-time RV living, the Escapees RV Club caters to a diverse community of RVers. With a strong emphasis on support and education, Escapees provides resources for those transitioning to full-time RV life. The club hosts events, including the annual Escapade, where members can forge connections and learn from experienced RVers.

3. Good Sam Club:

The Good Sam Club, affiliated with the Good Sam roadside assistance program, offers a wide range of benefits to its members. From campground discounts to travel assistance, the club is geared towards enhancing the RV lifestyle. Good Sam also organizes rallies and events, creating opportunities for members to socialize and network.

4. Airstream Club:

Airstream owners form a tight-knit community within the Airstream Club. This club is dedicated to the iconic silver bullet-shaped trailers. Members participate in caravans, rallies, and events designed specifically for Airstream enthusiasts, creating an environment where owners can share tips, stories, and a passion for these unique RVs.

5. RVillage:

RVillage is a social platform designed for RVers to connect both online and in-person. It allows members to join interest groups, share their travels, and find fellow RVers nearby. RVillage facilitates spontaneous meetups and gatherings, fostering a sense of community among RV enthusiasts on the road.

6. Full-Time Families:

Catering to families embracing the full-time RV lifestyle, Full-Time Families provides support, resources, and a sense of community. The club organizes rallies and events where families can connect, children can socialize, and parents can share insights on the unique challenges and joys of full-time RVing with kids.

7. Sisters on the Fly:

Sisters on the Fly is a unique club that celebrates the adventurous spirit of women in the RV community. This all-female club organizes gatherings and events where members can bond over outdoor activities, fishing, and the shared love of the open road.

8. Xscapers:

Xscapers, a sub-community within the Escapees RV Club, caters to a younger demographic of RVers, including working-age professionals and digital nomads. Xscapers organizes convergences, which are events designed for remote workers and those seeking a balance between work and travel.

9. RVing Women:

RVing Women is a supportive community for solo women RVers or those traveling without a partner. The club offers resources, educational opportunities, and organized events where women can connect, share experiences, and form lasting friendships.

10. Vintage Trailer Enthusiasts:

Enthusiasts of vintage trailers find a community in clubs like Tin Can Tourists and Vintage Airstream Club. These clubs celebrate the nostalgia and uniqueness of vintage RVs through rallies, restoration tips, and a shared appreciation for the history of RV travel.

In conclusion, RV clubs and gatherings are integral to the RVing lifestyle, providing a platform for enthusiasts to come together, share knowledge, and build lasting connections. Whether you're a full-time RVer, a weekend warrior, or someone with a specific RV type preference, there's likely a club or gathering tailored to your interests within the vibrant and supportive RV community.

Book 12: Environmental Responsibility

Leave No Trace Principles

The Leave No Trace principles is crucial for RV enthusiasts to ensure responsible and sustainable exploration of the great outdoors. These principles guide individuals to minimize their impact on the environment, preserve natural beauty, and contribute to the long-term health of ecosystems. Whether camping in remote locations or staying at established campgrounds, incorporating these principles into your RVing lifestyle is essential for environmental conservation.

1. Plan Ahead and Prepare:

Thorough planning is the first step toward responsible RVing. Research and choose campsites that can accommodate your RV, adhering to campground rules and regulations. This proactive approach minimizes the likelihood of encountering issues and ensures a seamless and environmentally conscious camping experience.

2. Travel and Camp on Durable Surfaces:

Stick to established roads and campsites to avoid damaging delicate ecosystems. RVers should refrain from creating new trails or camping in undesignated areas. Staying on durable surfaces helps protect vegetation and prevents erosion, preserving the natural beauty of the landscapes for future generations.

3. Dispose of Waste Properly:

Responsible waste disposal is a cornerstone of Leave No Trace ethics. RVers should utilize designated waste disposal facilities at campgrounds and RV parks. Avoid dumping gray or black water on the ground, as this can contaminate soil and water sources. Proper disposal ensures a clean and healthy environment for both people and wildlife.

4. Leave What You Find:

Preserving the integrity of natural landscapes is essential. Avoid picking plants, disturbing wildlife, or altering natural features. By leaving everything as you found it, you contribute to the conservation of biodiversity and maintain the ecological balance of the areas you explore.

5. Minimize Campfire Impact:

If campfires are allowed, adhere to established fire regulations and use existing fire rings. Keep fires small and manageable, using only dead and downed wood. Completely extinguish fires before leaving to prevent the risk of wildfires. Opting for a portable propane fire pit is a low-impact alternative.

6. Respect Wildlife:

Observe wildlife from a distance and avoid approaching or feeding them. Human interference can disrupt natural behaviors and habits, endangering both the animals and RVers. Maintaining a respectful distance ensures the well-being of wildlife populations and enhances the overall outdoor experience.

7. Be Considerate of Other Visitors:

Practicing courtesy toward fellow campers and outdoor enthusiasts contributes to a positive and harmonious environment. Keep noise levels to a minimum, respect privacy, and adhere to campground rules. Being considerate fosters a sense of community among RVers and ensures everyone can enjoy the tranquility of the outdoors.

8. Educate Yourself and Others:

Continuously educate yourself on Leave No Trace principles and share this knowledge with fellow RVers. By raising awareness about responsible RVing practices, you contribute to a collective effort to minimize the environmental impact of recreational vehicle travel.

Incorporating Leave No Trace principles into your RVing lifestyle goes beyond compliance; it reflects a commitment to environmental stewardship. By following these guidelines, RV enthusiasts can enjoy the beauty of nature while actively participating in its preservation. The Leave No Trace ethos not only ensures the protection of ecosystems but also fosters a shared responsibility among the RV community to leave the great outdoors as pristine as they found it.

Eco-Friendly RV Practices

Eco-friendly RV practices is essential for minimizing the ecological footprint of recreational vehicle travel and contributing to environmental sustainability. As the popularity of RVing continues to grow, adopting environmentally conscious habits becomes increasingly important. Here are tips for RV enthusiasts to reduce their impact on the environment and enjoy a more sustainable journey:

1. Solar Power and Energy Efficiency:

Invest in solar panels for your RV to harness the power of the sun for electricity. Solar energy can charge batteries, run appliances, and reduce reliance on traditional power sources. Additionally, focus on energy-efficient appliances and LED lighting to minimize energy consumption.

2. Water Conservation:

Practice water conservation by fixing any leaks in your RV plumbing and investing in water-saving fixtures. Use water-saving showerheads, faucets, and toilets to reduce water consumption. Collect rainwater for non-potable uses such as cleaning or watering plants.

3. Waste Reduction and Recycling:

Minimize waste by adopting a "reduce, reuse, recycle" approach. Opt for reusable items, such as water bottles and containers, to limit single-use plastics. Recycle materials like glass, plastic, and paper when facilities are available. Composting organic waste is another eco-friendly practice.

4. Sustainable Camping Practices:

Choose campgrounds that prioritize sustainability and eco-friendly initiatives. Many campgrounds are implementing recycling programs, energy-efficient facilities, and environmentally conscious landscaping. Supporting these initiatives contributes to a more sustainable RVing experience.

5. Responsible Chemical Use:

Select environmentally friendly cleaning products and toiletries to minimize the use of harmful chemicals. Avoid dumping chemical-based cleaning agents into natural water sources, and choose biodegradable options whenever possible. This reduces the impact on aquatic ecosystems.

6. Adopt Minimalist Living:

Embrace a minimalist lifestyle by decluttering and carrying only the essentials. The lighter your RV, the better its fuel efficiency, contributing to reduced carbon emissions. Simplifying your possessions also aligns with eco-conscious principles of consuming less.

7. Stay Longer, Travel Slower:

Instead of constant movement, consider staying longer at each destination. Traveling at a slower pace not only allows you to immerse yourself in local cultures but also reduces fuel consumption. Spend more time enjoying the surroundings and less time on the road.

8. Offset Carbon Footprint:

Consider participating in carbon offset programs to neutralize the environmental impact of your RV travels. These programs invest in initiatives like reforestation or renewable energy projects, effectively balancing the carbon emissions associated with your journey.

9. Eco-Friendly Driving Habits:

Adopt eco-friendly driving habits to enhance fuel efficiency. Maintain your RV's engine, drive at moderate speeds, and avoid unnecessary idling. Proper tire maintenance is also crucial for fuel economy.

10. Support Sustainable Tourism Initiatives:

Choose to patronize businesses and attractions that prioritize sustainable and eco-friendly practices. Supporting environmentally conscious establishments encourages the broader tourism industry to adopt greener initiatives.

By incorporating these eco-friendly RV practices into your journey, you can significantly reduce your environmental impact and contribute to the preservation of the natural beauty you encounter on the road. The collective effort of RV enthusiasts adopting sustainable habits is instrumental in ensuring that future generations can continue to enjoy the diverse landscapes that make RV travel a unique and enriching experience.

Book 13: Overcoming Challenges

Common Challenges

RV travel, while immensely rewarding, comes with its set of challenges that enthusiasts often encounter on the road. Overcoming these challenges requires a combination of preparation, adaptability, and a positive mindset. Here are some common challenges faced during RV travel and strategies to navigate through them:

1. Mechanical Issues:

RVs are complex machines, and mechanical issues can arise unexpectedly. Regular maintenance and pre-trip inspections are crucial to minimizing breakdowns. Carry essential tools, spare parts, and have a reliable roadside assistance plan to address unforeseen mechanical issues promptly.

2. Limited Amenities in Remote Areas:

Traveling to remote or less developed areas may limit access to amenities such as water, electricity, and waste disposal. Plan accordingly by conserving resources, investing in solar power for off-grid energy, and carrying extra water and fuel supplies. Be prepared for boondocking (camping without hookups) to enjoy more secluded locations.

3. Weather Challenges:

Weather conditions can be unpredictable and pose challenges to RVers. Extreme temperatures, storms, or heavy rain can impact travel plans. Stay informed about weather forecasts, plan routes accordingly, and have backup plans in case weather conditions become unfavorable. Pack appropriately for different climates.

4. Limited Storage Space:

RV living requires downsizing, and limited storage space can be a challenge. Optimize storage by using collapsible and multi-functional items. Prioritize essential items and be mindful of weight limits. Regularly declutter to maintain a comfortable and organized living space.

5. Connectivity Issues:

While the desire to disconnect is part of the RV experience, staying connected is essential for safety and remote work. Invest in signal boosters or portable Wi-Fi solutions to improve connectivity. Plan stops in areas with reliable cell service for essential communication.

6. Navigation Challenges:

RV navigation can be challenging, especially in unfamiliar territories. Invest in RV-specific GPS systems that consider the size and height of your vehicle. Plan routes in advance, double-checking for low-clearance bridges or restricted roads that may be unsuitable for RVs.

7. Waste Management:

Proper waste disposal can be a challenge, especially in areas without designated facilities. Learn about dump station locations, practice responsible waste disposal, and consider carrying a portable waste tank for added convenience. Utilize eco-friendly camping practices to minimize environmental impact.

8. Finding Pet-Friendly Spaces:

Traveling with pets adds another layer of consideration. While many RV parks are pet-friendly, not all destinations may be suitable for animals. Research pet-friendly attractions and parks in advance, carry necessary supplies, and ensure your pet is comfortable during travel.

9. Balancing Work and Leisure:

For those working remotely, finding a balance between work and leisure can be challenging. Establish a dedicated workspace in your RV, set realistic work hours, and plan leisure activities during downtime. Prioritize a healthy work-life balance to fully enjoy the RV lifestyle.

10. Community Dynamics in RV Parks:

While RV parks offer a sense of community, navigating different personalities can be challenging. Respect fellow RVers' space, follow campground etiquette, and participate in organized events to foster positive interactions. A friendly and considerate approach can enhance the community experience.

By acknowledging and proactively addressing these common challenges, RV enthusiasts can create a more enjoyable and fulfilling travel experience. Flexibility, preparation, and a willingness to adapt are key to overcoming the hurdles that may arise on the open road. With the right mindset and a sense of adventure, RV travel becomes a transformative journey despite its occasional challenges.

Emergency Preparedness

Emergency preparedness is a crucial aspect of RV travel, ensuring the safety and well-being of both travelers and their vehicles. Being on the road introduces unique challenges, and having a comprehensive plan in place can make a significant difference in handling emergencies. Here are key pieces of advice for RV enthusiasts to navigate unexpected situations:

1. First Aid Kit:

Every RV should be equipped with a well-stocked first aid kit. Include essentials like bandages, antiseptic wipes, pain relievers, and any necessary prescription medications. Regularly check the kit for expired items and replenish supplies as needed.

2. Emergency Contacts and Information:

Maintain a list of emergency contacts, including family members, friends, and healthcare providers. Include important medical information, insurance details, and a list of medications. Keep this information easily accessible in case of an emergency.

3. Communication Tools:

Ensure reliable communication tools are on hand. A fully charged cell phone with backup power, a two-way radio, or a satellite phone can be invaluable during emergencies. Familiarize yourself with local emergency numbers and coverage areas.

4. Vehicle Inspection and Maintenance:

Regularly inspect and maintain your RV to minimize the risk of breakdowns. Check tire pressure, fluid levels, and the condition of brakes and lights. Address any issues promptly to avoid potential emergencies on the road.

5. Weather Preparedness:

Stay informed about weather conditions along your route. Be prepared for sudden changes in weather, especially in regions prone to severe weather events. Have appropriate clothing, emergency blankets, and extra supplies to endure unexpected weather challenges.

6. Emergency Roadside Assistance:

Enroll in a reliable roadside assistance program specific to RVs. These services can provide towing, tire replacement, fuel delivery, and other assistance. Having a plan in place ensures quick and efficient help in case of vehicle-related emergencies.

7. Fire Safety:

Implement fire safety measures in your RV. Install smoke detectors and carbon monoxide alarms, and test them regularly. Have a fire extinguisher on hand and know how to use it. Establish an evacuation plan in case of a fire emergency.

8. Navigation and Maps:

Always have a paper map or atlas as a backup to your electronic navigation tools. In areas with poor signal reception, a physical map can be a lifesaver. Familiarize yourself with alternative routes in case your planned route is obstructed.

9. Campground Safety Awareness:

When staying in campgrounds, be aware of the location of emergency exits, fire hydrants, and first aid stations. Familiarize yourself with the campground's emergency procedures and communicate them to your travel companions.

10. Community Support:

Foster a sense of community with fellow RVers. In case of emergencies, neighbors can provide valuable assistance and support. Participate in campground activities and events to build connections that may prove beneficial during challenging times.

11. Remote Location Considerations:

If planning to venture into remote areas, assess the availability of emergency services and plan accordingly. Carry extra water, food, and fuel, and inform someone of your itinerary. Satellite communication devices can be crucial in areas with limited cell coverage.

12. Stay Calm and Assess:

In any emergency, staying calm is paramount. Assess the situation, prioritize safety, and follow the established emergency plan. Panicking can hinder effective decision-making and exacerbate the situation.

By prioritizing emergency preparedness, RV enthusiasts can enjoy their travels with greater peace of mind. While it's impossible to predict every scenario, a well-thought-out plan and the right resources can make a significant difference in handling emergencies on the road.

Book 14: Exploring Top America's Campgrounds

(Photo of www.pexel.com)

When embarking on the monumental task of curating the top campgrounds for RV enthusiasts to explore across the United States, a robust and thoughtful selection process is imperative. The diversity and richness of the American landscape offer a vast array of camping experiences, from serene lakeside retreats to rugged mountain hideaways. In "The Lost RV Camping Bible," the selection of campgrounds is meticulously crafted, ensuring that each location provides an unparalleled opportunity to connect with nature, embark on outdoor adventures, and create lasting memories. The criteria for selection are rooted in location, amenities, reviews, and unique features, offering a comprehensive guide that caters to a wide range of preferences and camping styles.

Location: The essence of any great camping experience begins with its location. The campgrounds selected for this guide are strategically spread across various geographical landscapes of the United States, ensuring that travelers can find a stunning destination no matter where their journey takes them. From the awe-inspiring vistas of the Grand Canyon to the tranquil shores of the Great Lakes, each campground's location is chosen for its ability to offer something truly special—a unique backdrop for adventure and relaxation.

Amenities: For many RV travelers, the quality and range of amenities available at a campground significantly influence their stay. High-quality restrooms and showers, full-service RV hookups, laundry facilities, and Wi-Fi are among the essential amenities that can transform a good camping experience into a great one. Additional amenities like swimming pools, recreation rooms, and on-site convenience stores further enhance the camping experience, providing comfort and convenience. The guide prioritizes campgrounds that strike the perfect balance between embracing the rustic charm of the outdoors and offering modern comforts that cater to the needs of today's RVers.

Reviews: In the age of digital information, reviews from fellow travelers play a critical role in the selection process. They offer genuine insights into the camping experience, highlighting both the highs and lows. Campgrounds included in this guide boast positive reviews across multiple platforms, reflecting their commitment to quality, hospitality, and visitor satisfaction. These reviews serve as a testament to the campground's ability to meet and exceed the expectations of a diverse community of campers, ensuring that the recommendations are based on real experiences and trusted feedback.

Unique Features: Beyond the conventional criteria, the allure of a campground often lies in its unique features—those elements that set it apart from the rest. Whether it's the opportunity to camp under the stars in a Dark Sky Park, access to exceptional hiking trails, or the chance to partake in local cultural activities, these unique features contribute significantly to the selection. The guide seeks out campgrounds that offer something truly special, whether through their environmental initiatives, cultural significance, or simply an unparalleled location that offers breathtaking views and experiences.

By meticulously evaluating each campground against these criteria, "The Lost RV Camping Bible" aspires to provide RV travelers with an authoritative and inspiring guide to the best camping experiences across the United States. The aim is not just to list destinations but to curate journeys that inspire adventure, foster connections with nature, and encourage exploration of the incredible diversity of the American outdoors. Each selected campground promises to elevate the RV living dream, ensuring that every stop on the road is not just a place to park but a memorable chapter in the grand adventure of life.

Special Features of Selected Campgrounds

Under Canvas Zion - Utah

Nestled beside the majestic Zion National Park, Under Canvas Zion offers a luxurious camping experience that combines the thrill of the outdoors with the comforts of a boutique hotel. This glamping site's use of safari-inspired tents equipped with king-size beds, wood-burning stoves, and private bathrooms provides an unparalleled camping experience. Its unique accommodations allow guests to immerse themselves in the natural beauty of Zion's red cliffs and star-filled skies while enjoying high-end amenities. Special features include guided tours, outdoor yoga, and an on-site restaurant, making it an exceptional base for exploring Zion National Park's sprawling deserts and towering rock formations.

Treebones Resort - Big Sur, California

Perched along the wild Pacific coast, Treebones Resort offers a unique way to experience the stunning beauty of Big Sur. This eco-friendly resort features yurts, autonomous tents, and the famous Human Nest - a woven wood art piece that functions as a sleeping space. Guests can enjoy unparalleled views of the ocean, hike in the surrounding wilderness, or visit nearby attractions like the Hearst Castle and Julia Pfeiffer Burns State Park. The resort's commitment to sustainability, organic architecture, and local cuisine highlights the special connection between luxury and the natural environment.

Dry Tortugas National Park - Florida

Accessible only by boat or seaplane, camping at Dry Tortugas National Park offers a remote island experience unlike any other in the United States. Situated in the Gulf of Mexico, the park is known for its crystal-clear waters, coral reefs, and the historic Fort Jefferson. Campers can enjoy snorkeling, bird watching, and exploring the fort's massive walls and moats. The isolation of Dry Tortugas ensures a peaceful camping experience with spectacu

lar stargazing opportunities, making it a special destination for those looking to escape the hustle and bustle of the mainland.

Havasu Falls Campground - Supai, Arizona

Havasu Falls Campground is a breathtaking oasis located in the Grand Canyon's rugged terrain. The campground is near the Havasupai Indian Reservation and is famous for its turquoise waterfalls cascading into travertine swimming holes. The journey to the campground involves a 10-mile hike, ensuring that visitors are adventurers at heart. The effort is rewarded with the opportunity to swim in some of the most stunning natural pools in the world, surrounded by the red rock walls of the canyon. The campground's proximity to such extraordinary natural beauty makes it a bucket-list destination for many.

Whitepod Eco-Luxury Hotel - Swiss Alps

While not in the US, Whitepod Eco-Luxury Hotel in the Swiss Alps deserves mention for its innovative approach to camping. Set against the backdrop of the majestic Alps, Whitepod offers geodesic domes with luxury bedding, wood-burning stoves, and full bathrooms. This eco-friendly resort emphasizes minimal environmental impact while providing a comfortable base for exploring the surrounding mountains. Activities include hiking, skiing, and paragliding, making it a unique blend of adventure and luxury.

The Enchanted Rock State Natural Area - Texas

The Enchanted Rock State Natural Area offers camping near an ancient pink granite dome rising above Central Texas. This geological wonder is not only a magnet for hikers and rock climbers but also holds a special place in Native American folklore. The park's night skies are another highlight, offering some of the best stargazing in Texas due to its designation as an International Dark Sky Park. Camping here allows visitors to connect with both the natural world and the rich cultural history of the area.

Jumbo Rocks Campground - Joshua Tree National Park, California

Situated among the park's iconic bouldered landscapes, Jumbo Rocks Campground offers a unique camping experience in Joshua Tree National Park. The campground is named for its massive rock formations, providing a dramatic backdrop for camping and climbing enthusiasts. Its location also offers easy access to key park attractions like Skull Rock. The stark beauty of the desert, combined with the surreal Joshua Trees and star-filled night skies, makes this campground a special destination for nature lovers and photographers.

Glacier Bay's Bartlett Cove Campground - Alaska

Located within Glacier Bay National Park, Bartlett Cove Campground offers an immersive experience in Alaska's wild beauty. Campers can explore glaciers, watch for whales and bears, and kayak in pristine waters. The campground's proximity to the park's visitor center and guided tours makes it an excellent base for learning about the region's ecology and indigenous cultures. The unparalleled natural beauty and opportunities for adventure highlight the special qualities of camping in Alaska.

Skycamp - Shenandoah Valley, Virginia

Nestled in the rolling hills of the Shenandoah Valley, Skycamp offers a unique treehouse camping experience that blends adventure with the tranquility of forest living. Elevated platforms amidst the hardwoods provide a bird's-eye view of the surrounding natural beauty, while the proximity to Shenandoah National Park allows for easy exploration of its extensive trail network and stunning vistas. Skycamp's commitment to sustainable tourism and providing a secluded retreat makes it a special destination for those looking to connect with nature in a novel way.

Minnewaska State Park Reserve - New York

Perched atop the Shawangunk Ridge, Minnewaska State Park Reserve offers camping near crystal-clear sky lakes, towering waterfalls, and rugged, rocky terrain. The park's unique geological features and its network of well-maintained trails attract hikers, bikers, and rock climbers seeking a challenge amidst breathtaking scenery. Camping here means waking up to serene lake views and ending days with stunning sunsets, making it a standout destination for nature enthusiasts looking for beauty both above and below the horizon.

El Cosmico - Marfa, Texas

El Cosmico is a nomadic hotel and campground in the artsy town of Marfa, offering a unique blend of artistic culture and camping. With accommodations ranging from vintage trailers and tepees to safari tents and yurts, El Cosmico provides a bohemian camping experience unlike any other. The site's communal spaces, outdoor baths, and hammock grove encourage interaction among travelers, fostering a sense of community. Its location in the West Texas desert offers spectacular night skies, making it a special place for stargazers and those seeking a creative retreat.

Devils Tower KOA - Wyoming

Situated in the shadow of America's first national monument, Devils Tower KOA offers an unforgettable camping experience. The campground's proximity to the awe-inspiring geological feature allows for easy exploration of the tower's massive columns and the surrounding prairie. Special amenities include an on-site movie theater showing "Close Encounters of the Third Kind" nightly, enhancing the mystical allure of camping near this iconic landmark. The blend of natural wonder, cultural significance, and unique entertainment options makes Devils Tower KOA a special spot for campers.

Lakedale Resort at Three Lakes - San Juan Islands, Washington

Lakedale Resort offers a luxury camping experience on San Juan Island, featuring canvas cabins with lake views, plush bedding, and fire pits. The resort's location amidst three freshwater lakes provides ample opportunities for fishing, kayaking, and paddleboarding. The beauty of the San Juan Islands, with their abundant wildlife and scenic vistas, is easily accessible from this campground. Lakedale's blend of outdoor activities, resort amenities, and the tranquility of island life creates a unique and memorable camping experience.

Bluewater Key RV Resort - Florida Keys

Bluewater Key offers a taste of paradise with its luxury RV sites located just off the iconic Overseas Highway. Each private site is landscaped for privacy and equipped with tiki huts and docks, providing direct access to the clear blue waters of the Florida Keys. The resort's amenities, including a temperature-controlled swimming pool and dog park, cater to a comfortable and indulgent camping experience. Its location near Key West allows for exploration of the area's vibrant culture, historic sites, and water-based activities, making Bluewater Key a special destination for those seeking sun, sea, and luxury.

The Pines Resort - Yosemite National Park, California

Offering a serene retreat in the Sierra Nevada Mountains, The Pines Resort at Yosemite combines the beauty of wilderness camping with the comforts of resort accommodations. Nestled among towering pines and within close proximity to Yosemite's iconic landmarks, the resort offers cabins, yurts, and traditional campsite options. The special feature of The Pines is its accessibility to Yosemite's majestic waterfalls, deep valleys, and ancient giant sequoias, providing an unparalleled base for exploring one of America's most beloved national parks.

Ohiopyle State Park - Pennsylvania

Ohiopyle State Park is a haven for outdoor enthusiasts, offering access to some of the best whitewater rafting in the eastern United States. The Youghiogheny River provides thrilling rapids for rafting and kayaking, while miles of hiking and biking trails offer more serene ways to explore the park's scenic beauty. The campground itself offers basic amenities, allowing campers to immerse themselves in the natural surroundings. Its special feature lies in its proximity to the breathtaking Ohiopyle Falls and the surrounding Laurel Highlands, a landscape of rolling hills, lush forests, and historic sites.

Mather Campground - Grand Canyon National Park, Arizona

Located on the South Rim of the Grand Canyon, Mather Campground offers campers the opportunity to stay within one of the world's most iconic landscapes. The campground provides a comfortable, family-friendly base from which to explore the park's vast network of trails, viewpoints, and educational programs. The unmatched beauty of the Grand Canyon, with its layered bands of red rock revealing millions of years of geological history, is the campground's most compelling feature. The proximity to scenic vistas like Mather Point and Yavapai Observation Station makes this campground a special destination for those looking to experience the grandeur of the Grand Canyon up close.

Watchman Campground - Zion National Park, Utah

Strategically located near the park's main visitor center, Watchman Campground is an ideal base for exploring Zion National Park's towering cliffs, narrow canyons, and river valleys. The campground's sites offer views of the Watchman Peak, providing a stunning backdrop for your stay. Easy access to the park's shuttle service allows campers to explore the main attractions without the hassle of parking. The nearby Virgin River offers refreshing swimming holes and the start of the park's famous Narrows hike. Its special features include the convenience and natural beauty that make it a memorable spot for adventurers and families alike.

Acadia National Park - Blackwoods Campground, Maine

Blackwoods Campground offers a gateway to the rugged coastlines, dense woodlands, and mountainous terrain of Acadia National Park. Located on Mount Desert Island, the campground provides easy access to the park's top attractions, including Cadillac Mountain, Jordan Pond, and the Park Loop Road. The dense forests around the campground offer a sense of seclusion, while the proximity to Bar Harbor provides convenient access to shops and restaurants. The special feature of Blackwoods is its blend of accessibility to both natural wonders and local amenities, offering a comprehensive Acadia experience.

Assateague Island National Seashore - Maryland & Virginia

Camping on Assateague Island brings a unique experience of waking up to the sight of wild horses roaming the beaches and dunes. This barrier island, split between Maryland and Virginia, offers sandy beaches, salt marshes, and coastal bays to explore. The sound of ocean waves serves as a constant backdrop to your camping adventure, with opportunities for swimming, kayaking, and beachcombing. The island's dynamic landscape, shaped by wind and water, is constantly changing, providing a unique backdrop for photography and nature observation. The special feature of Assateague is the wild horses, along with the chance to camp in a pristine beach setting, making it an unforgettable destination for nature lovers.

Glacier National Park - Many Glacier Campground, Montana

Many Glacier Campground, nestled within the rugged Montana wilderness of Glacier National Park, is often referred to as the heart of the park due to its stunning scenery and abundant wildlife. This campground offers direct access to some of Glacier's most famous hikes, including the Grinnell Glacier Trail, where hikers can witness the effects of climate change on the park's receding glaciers. The special features of Many Glacier include the chance to see wildlife such as bears, moose, and bighorn sheep in their natural habitat, and the proximity to Swiftcurrent Lake, ideal for kayaking and canoeing amidst towering mountain peaks.

Yosemite National Park - Upper Pines Campground, California

Upper Pines Campground lies in the shadow of Half Dome and Yosemite Falls, offering campers a prime location from which to explore Yosemite National Park's awe-inspiring natural wonders. This campground provides easy access to the park's extensive trail network, including the Mist Trail, leading to the iconic Vernal and Nevada Falls. The special feature of Upper Pines is its combination of accessibility to Yosemite's most famous landmarks and the immersive experience of sleeping under the stars in one of America's most beloved national parks.

Olympic National Park - Hoh Rain Forest Campground, Washington

The Hoh Rain Forest Campground offers a unique camping experience in one of the largest temperate rainforests in the United States. This lush, green environment is home to towering old-growth trees, mosses, and ferns, creating a fairy-tale setting. The campground serves as a starting point for exploring the Hoh Rain

Forest's network of trails, including the Hall of Mosses and the Hoh River Trail. Its special feature is the opportunity to camp in an environment that feels worlds away from the typical camping experience, offering a serene and mystical retreat into nature.

Great Smoky Mountains National Park - Cades Cove Campground, Tennessee

Cades Cove Campground sits in a verdant valley surrounded by the majestic Smoky Mountains, providing campers with panoramic views and the chance to spot wildlife such as white-tailed deer, black bears, and wild turkeys. The campground is a starting point for exploring Cades Cove, one of the park's most popular destinations, on a scenic loop road that offers access to historic buildings, hiking trails, and stunning mountain vistas. The special feature of Cades Cove is the blend of natural beauty, wildlife viewing opportunities, and historical exploration, making it a comprehensive camping experience that captures the essence of the Great Smoky Mountains.

Arches National Park - Devils Garden Campground, Utah

Devils Garden Campground offers an immersive experience in the heart of Arches National Park, surrounded by the park's iconic red rock formations and arches. This campground provides easy access to the Devils Garden Trailhead, leading to a series of spectacular arches, including Landscape Arch, one of the longest natural arches in the world. The special feature of camping at Devils Garden is the opportunity to explore these geological wonders up close, with the added bonus of experiencing unforgettable stargazing in one of the most pristine night skies in America.

Big Sur Campground & Cabins, California

Nestled among the towering redwoods along California's scenic Highway 1, Big Sur Campground & Cabins provides a magical escape into one of the state's most breathtaking coastal regions. This family-friendly campground offers a mix of tent camping sites, RV spots, and rustic cabins, all within earshot of the Big Sur River. Special features include inner tubing on the river, a playground for children, and the proximity to iconic Big Sur landmarks like Pfeiffer Beach and McWay Falls. The blend of coastal beauty, forested surroundings, and accessible outdoor activities makes this campground a special haven for those seeking to experience the rugged charm of Big Sur.

Dry Tortugas National Park - Garden Key Campground, Florida

As one of the most remote national parks in the United States, Dry Tortugas offers a truly unique camping experience on Garden Key, accessible only by boat or seaplane from Key West. The campground is situated near historic Fort Jefferson, a massive 19th-century fortress that offers fascinating tours. Special features of camping at Dry Tortugas include snorkeling in crystal-clear waters teeming with vibrant marine life, stargazing free from light pollution, and the sense of isolation and tranquility that comes from being miles away from the mainland. This campground is a special destination for those looking to disconnect and immerse themselves in the natural and historical wonders of this remote island paradise.

Canyonlands National Park - Willow Flat Campground, Utah

Willow Flat Campground, located in the Island in the Sky district of Canyonlands National Park, offers a secluded and primitive camping experience amidst Utah's dramatic desert landscape. With only 12 sites, this campground provides an intimate setting for enjoying the park's sweeping vistas, deep canyons, and towering mesas. The campground's special feature is its proximity to the Green River Overlook and Mesa Arch, two of the park's most iconic viewpoints, offering spectacular sunrise and sunset views. Camping at Willow Flat is ideal for those seeking solitude and a deep connection with the rugged beauty of Canyonlands.

Acadia National Park - Seawall Campground, Maine

Seawall Campground is located on the quieter side of Mount Desert Island, offering a peaceful retreat within Acadia National Park. This campground is a short walk from the rocky shores of the Atlantic Ocean, where campers can explore tide pools, watch for seabirds, and enjoy the sound of waves crashing against the coastline. Special features include close proximity to the Wonderland Trail and Bass Harbor Head Lighthouse, as well as the opportunity to participate in ranger-led programs. Seawall Campground provides a serene base for exploring Acadia's diverse landscapes, from coastal areas to forested trails and mountain peaks.

Glacier National Park - Two Medicine Campground, Montana

Two Medicine Campground, located in the less-visited southeastern part of Glacier National Park, offers a tranquil camping experience surrounded by stunning mountain scenery. This area of the park is known for its spectacular hikes, pristine lakes, and abundant wildlife. The campground's special features include easy access to Two Medicine Lake, where campers can rent boats or embark on scenic boat tours, and the chance to hike to iconic locations like Trick Falls and Upper Two Medicine Lake. Two Medicine Campground is a special retreat for those seeking to experience the natural beauty and tranquility of Glacier National Park away from the crowds.

North Cascades National Park - Colonial Creek Campground, Washington

In the heart of the North Cascades, Colonial Creek Campground sits on the shores of Diablo Lake, renowned for its vivid turquoise waters. The campground is an ideal base for exploring the surrounding wilderness, offering access to trails that range from leisurely walks to challenging hikes into the alpine landscape. Special features of Colonial Creek include canoeing and kayaking on Diablo Lake, where campers can paddle among towering peaks, and proximity to the North Cascades Environmental Learning Center, offering educational programs about the region's ecology. This campground is a special haven for those seeking both adventure and insight into the natural world.

Great Sand Dunes National Park and Preserve - Piñon Flats Campground, Colorado

Piñon Flats is a campground that offers a unique experience in the shadow of North America's tallest sand dunes. Located in Great Sand Dunes National Park and Preserve, this campground provides visitors with the opportunity to explore this unique landscape of dunes, forests, and mountains. Special features include sand sledding and boarding, night sky programs, and access to Medano Creek, a seasonal stream ideal for cooling off after a day of adventure. Camping at Piñon Flats offers a distinctive blend of activities that can't be found in any other national park.

Shenandoah National Park - Big Meadows Campground, Virginia

Big Meadows Campground, situated within Shenandoah National Park, is known for its large, open meadow, which is a hub for wildlife viewing, especially deer and the occasional black bear. The campground provides easy access to some of the park's most scenic hiking trails, including the Appalachian Trail and trails to waterfalls and panoramic overlooks. Special features of Big Meadows include the nearby Byrd Visitor Center, offering educational exhibits and ranger programs, and the spectacular display of wildflowers in spring and summer. This campground is a special destination for those who appreciate both the beauty and the biodiversity of the Appalachian Mountains.

Redwood National and State Parks - Jedediah Smith Campground, California

Nestled among towering old-growth redwoods, Jedediah Smith Campground offers an immersive experience in one of the most majestic forests on Earth. Located in Redwood National and State Parks, the campground is near the Smith River, California's last major free-flowing river, which provides opportunities for swimming, fishing, and kayaking. Special features include access to the Stout Grove, a short walk from the campground, where visitors can stand among some of the tallest trees in the world. This campground is a special retreat for those seeking tranquility and a deep connection with ancient natural wonders.

Joshua Tree National Park - Indian Cove Campground, California

Indian Cove Campground is nestled among the iconic boulder formations of Joshua Tree National Park, offering a unique desert camping experience. The campground provides access to a variety of rock climbing routes, making it a popular destination for climbers. Special features include the nature trail that winds through the cove, offering up-close encounters with the park's namesake Joshua trees and other desert flora. The campground's location also makes it ideal for stargazing, away from the light pollution of nearby cities. Indian Cove offers a special opportunity to immerse oneself in the stark beauty and silence of the Mojave Desert.

Katmai National Park & Preserve - Brooks Camp Campground, Alaska

Brooks Camp Campground in Katmai National Park & Preserve offers an unparalleled wilderness experience in the remote Alaskan landscape. This campground is world-renowned for its bear viewing opportunities, as it's situated near Brooks River, a prime spot for brown bears to catch salmon. Special features include the bear viewing platforms, which allow visitors to safely observe these magnificent creatures in their natural habitat. Additionally, the proximity to the Valley of Ten Thousand Smokes, an ash-filled valley formed by the Novarupta volcano's 1912 eruption, offers a unique geological exploration experience. This campground is a must-visit for wildlife enthusiasts and those seeking adventure in the Alaskan wilderness.

Voyageurs National Park - Kettle Falls Campground, Minnesota

Kettle Falls Campground is uniquely accessible only by water, nestled in Voyageurs National Park, a water-based park primarily located on the Minnesota-Canadian border. This location offers campers a chance to immerse themselves in the tranquility of the northern lakes, with opportunities for boating, fishing, and kayaking in the interconnected waterways of Rainy, Kabetogama, Namakan, and Sand Point Lakes. The campground's special features include its proximity to the historic Kettle Falls Hotel and the picturesque views of the waterfalls for which it is named. This destination is ideal for those looking to escape into the serenity of the northern wilderness and enjoy the peacefulness of lake life.

Cuyahoga Valley National Park - Stanford Backcountry Campsites, Ohio

Stanford Backcountry Campsites in Cuyahoga Valley National Park offer a unique backcountry camping experience within the boundaries of an urban national park. These campsites provide a secluded retreat amidst the rolling hills and forests of Ohio, with access to the park's extensive network of trails, including the Towpath Trail that follows the historic Ohio & Erie Canal. Special features of this camping experience include the proximity to Brandywine Falls, a stunning 65-foot waterfall, and the chance to explore the cultural heritage of the Ohio & Erie Canal. This campground is perfect for those seeking a wilderness experience with the convenience of nearby urban amenities.

White Mountain National Forest - Hancock Campground, New Hampshire

Hancock Campground is located in the heart of the White Mountain National Forest, offering campers easy access to the scenic beauty and outdoor adventures of New Hampshire's White Mountains. This campground is ideal for those interested in hiking, with trails leading to Franconia Notch and the Lincoln Woods. Special features include the campground's location along the East Branch of the Pemigewasset River, providing a serene backdrop and opportunities for fishing and swimming. The rustic charm and natural beauty of Hancock Campground make it a special destination for campers seeking to explore the rugged landscapes of the Northeast.

Everglades National Park - Flamingo Campground, Florida

Flamingo Campground offers a gateway to the unique and diverse ecosystems of Everglades National Park, the largest subtropical wilderness in the United States. Located at the southern tip of the Florida peninsula, this campground provides opportunities for wildlife viewing, including alligators, manatees, and a plethora of bird species. Special features include access to canoe and kayak trails through the mangroves, guided boat tours, and the chance to witness the spectacular sunsets over Florida Bay. This campground is a special spot for nature lovers and those interested in the conservation and exploration of the Everglades' unique ecosystems.

Sequoia National Park - Lodgepole Campground, California

Nestled in the Sierra Nevada mountains, Lodgepole Campground provides a base to explore the giant sequoias of Sequoia National Park. Near the towering General Sherman Tree, the world's largest tree by volume, this campground offers easy access to a network of trails leading through groves of ancient sequoias. Special features include the nearby Lodgepole Village with a visitor center, market, and shuttle service to other parts of the park. This campground is ideal for those who want to marvel at the majestic sequoias and explore the high sierra landscapes.

Black Canyon of the Gunnison National Park - South Rim Campground, Colorado

The South Rim Campground offers stunning views into the depths of Black Canyon of the Gunnison, one of North America's most dramatic and steep-walled canyons. With easy access to rim trails and the visitor center, campers can explore the canyon's unique geology and enjoy stargazing in some of the darkest skies in the United States. The special feature of this campground is its proximity to the Gunnison River, which offers excellent opportunities for fishing and observing the canyon's unique ecosystem. This destination is perfect for those interested in geology, astronomy, and experiencing the profound depth of one of America's most striking canyons.

Mount Rainier National Park - Cougar Rock Campground, Washington

Cougar Rock Campground, situated in the shadow of Mount Rainier, provides campers with easy access to the park's wildflower meadows, ancient forests, and glacier-fed rivers. This campground is a great starting point for exploring the Paradise area, known for its stunning vistas of Mount Rainier and miles of hiking trails through alpine landscapes. Special features include educational programs at the nearby Paradise Jackson Visitor Center and the breathtaking Narada Falls, just a short drive from the campground. Cougar Rock is an ideal spot for those wishing to explore the diverse ecosystems and awe-inspiring beauty of Mount Rainier National Park.

Grand Teton National Park - Signal Mountain Campground, Wyoming

Located on the shores of Jackson Lake with direct views of the Teton Range, Signal Mountain Campground offers a picturesque setting unmatched by any other. Campers can enjoy kayaking, fishing, and swimming in the lake, with easy access to the park's extensive trail system for hiking and wildlife viewing. The special feature of this campground is its location, providing unparalleled views of the Tetons and excellent opportunities for photography and wildlife observation. Signal Mountain is a must-visit for those who want to immerse themselves in the stunning landscapes and outdoor activities offered by Grand Teton National Park.

Acadia National Park - Duck Harbor Campground, Maine

Accessible only by mailboat from the town of Stonington, Duck Harbor Campground on Isle au Haut offers a remote island camping experience in Acadia National Park. This secluded campground provides a unique opportunity to explore the rugged coastline, wooded trails, and quiet solitude of Isle au Haut. Special features include the chance to disconnect and enjoy backcountry camping with ocean views, hiking along the island's cliffs, and observing the rich marine and bird life. Duck Harbor Campground is ideal for adventurers seeking a more isolated and intimate connection with Acadia's natural beauty.

Isle Royale National Park - Rock Harbor Campground, Michigan

Located on a remote island in Lake Superior, Rock Harbor Campground offers a unique wilderness experience in Isle Royale National Park. Accessible only by boat or seaplane, this campground serves as a gateway to exploring the island's rugged terrain, forested trails, and crystal-clear waters. Special features include kayaking along the shoreline, spotting moose and wolves that inhabit the island, and diving into the park's underwater shipwrecks. This destination is perfect for those seeking solitude and adventure in one of the most secluded and pristine natural environments in the United States.

Arapaho and Roosevelt National Forests - Guanella Pass Campground, Colorado

Guanella Pass Campground, nestled in the high country of the Colorado Rockies, offers breathtaking views of Mount Bierstadt and Mount Evans. This high-altitude campground is a base for hiking, fishing in Clear Creek, and exploring the scenic byway that traverses Guanella Pass. Special features include the stunning alpine scenery, opportunities for wildlife viewing, and access to numerous high-country trails. This campground is ideal for those looking to experience the rugged beauty and serenity of the Colorado wilderness.

Big Bend National Park - Chisos Basin Campground, Texas

Chisos Basin Campground sits in a natural amphitheater surrounded by volcanic rock cliffs in the heart of Big Bend National Park. At an elevation that offers cooler temperatures, this campground provides access to some of the park's most scenic hiking trails, including the Window Trail and the Lost Mine Trail. Special features include breathtaking sunsets through "The Window," a unique rock formation, and the chance to observe diverse wildlife, including black bears and mountain lions. This destination offers a mix of adventure and tranquility, perfect for exploring the diverse ecosystems and stunning landscapes of Big Bend.

Glacier National Park - Apgar Campground, Montana

Apgar Campground, located near the west entrance of Glacier National Park, offers easy access to Lake McDonald and Apgar Village. As one of the park's largest campgrounds, Apgar serves as a hub for activities such as boating, swimming, and fishing, with rental facilities available for kayaks and paddleboards. Special features include guided ranger programs, breathtaking views of the surrounding mountains, and proximity to the Going-to-the-Sun Road, offering easy access to the park's many natural wonders. Apgar Campground is ideal for families and first-time visitors looking to experience the majestic beauty of Glacier National Park.

Shenandoah National Park - Loft Mountain Campground, Virginia

Loft Mountain Campground, situated atop Big Flat Mountain, offers expansive views of the Blue Ridge Mountains and access to the Appalachian Trail. This campground is known for its beautiful sunrises and sunsets, ample opportunities for wildlife viewing, and a variety of hiking trails that range from easy walks to challenging treks. Special features include two waterfalls within walking distance and the chance to pick wild blueberries in late summer. Loft Mountain Campground is perfect for those who wish to immerse themselves in the peaceful beauty of the Appalachian Mountains and explore the scenic wonders of Shenandoah National Park.

Camping is a journey of continual discovery. There's always a new trail to explore, a new park to visit, or a new skill to master. Whether you're camping near home or trekking to remote destinations, each trip offers its own set of challenges and rewards. The experiences gained not only deepen our appreciation for the natural world but also teach valuable lessons in resilience, resourcefulness, and the simple joy of living in the moment.

As we look to the horizon, ready for our next outdoor adventure, let us remember the vast tapestry of campgrounds and natural wonders awaiting our exploration. The call of the wild is an invitation to step outside our everyday lives, to explore, learn, and grow. So lace up your boots, pack your bag, and set out on a journey to discover the boundless beauty and adventure that camping in the United States has to offer. The great outdoors is not just a destination but a pathway to discovery, connection, and the endless pursuit of the horizon..

Book 15: Reflecting on the Journey

Journaling and Documentation

Keeping a travel journal or documenting the RV journey through photos and videos is a delightful and enriching practice that enhances the RVing experience. Beyond the joy of reliving memories, these creative outlets serve as invaluable keepsakes, capturing the essence of the journey and preserving the unique moments encountered on the road.

1. Preserving Memories:

A travel journal acts as a personal chronicle of the RV adventure. Whether it's the stunning landscapes, the camaraderie of fellow travelers, or the unexpected encounters, a journal allows you to vividly recall the details of each experience. Documenting memories ensures they remain vivid and cherished for years to come.

2. Reflection and Gratitude:

Journaling provides an opportunity for reflection and gratitude. Take moments to jot down your thoughts, feelings, and the lessons learned during the journey. Expressing gratitude for the beauty of nature, the warmth of community, or the simple joys of RV living reinforces a positive mindset.

3. Creating a Travel Legacy:

Your travel journal becomes a legacy—a tangible record of your adventures that can be passed down through generations. Future family members or fellow RV enthusiasts may find inspiration and insight in your documented experiences. It becomes a gift of shared stories and wisdom.

4. Enhancing Self-Discovery:

Writing about your RV experiences allows for self-discovery. Explore your own reactions to new places, challenges faced, and personal growth. The journal becomes a mirror reflecting not only the external landscapes but also the internal landscapes of your journey.

5. Capturing Local Cultures:

Embrace the cultural richness of each destination by documenting local customs, cuisines, and traditions in your journal. Share anecdotes of encounters with locals, explore regional festivals, and describe the flavors of local cuisine. Your journal becomes a cultural mosaic of your travels.

6. Photo and Video Storytelling:

Complement your written journal with visual storytelling through photos and videos. Capture the breathtaking landscapes, candid moments, and the unique character of each place. These visuals not only serve as mementos but also allow you to share your journey with others in a vivid and engaging way.

7. Building Connections:

Sharing your travel experiences through a blog, social media, or a dedicated website fosters connections within the RV community. Others may find inspiration, advice, or camaraderie through your documented journey. It's a way to contribute to the collective tapestry of RV experiences.

8. Planning Future Adventures:

Reviewing your travel journal and revisiting photos and videos can inspire future adventures. Your documented experiences serve as a roadmap for planning return trips or exploring new destinations. It becomes a source of inspiration for continuous exploration.

9. Therapeutic Benefits:

Journaling has therapeutic benefits, providing a space for emotional expression and stress relief. During challenging times or unexpected detours, the act of writing can serve as a form of catharsis, helping you process emotions and maintain a positive outlook.

10. Creative Expression:

Keeping a travel journal allows for creative expression. Experiment with writing styles, include sketches, or add mementos like pressed flowers or ticket stubs. The journal becomes a canvas for your artistic inclinations, making the documentation process enjoyable and personal.

Whether in the form of words, images, or a combination of both, documenting your RV journey is a rewarding endeavor. It transforms the act of traveling into a holistic experience—one that is not just lived but also remembered, shared, and celebrated through the beautiful art of journaling and documentation.

Memorable Moments

Embarking on an RV journey opens the door to a myriad of unforgettable moments, each contributing to the tapestry of a unique and enriching experience on the road. From the awe-inspiring landscapes to the unexpected encounters with fellow travelers, these personal anecdotes and stories illuminate the essence of the RV lifestyle.

1. The Hidden Gem in the Desert:

While traversing the arid landscapes of the American Southwest, a chance detour led to the discovery of a hidden gem—a secluded desert oasis surrounded by towering red rocks. This unexpected find transformed a routine travel day into an extraordinary experience, complete with a refreshing dip in a natural hot spring under the vast desert sky.

2. Campfire Conversations:

One of the most cherished memories was an impromptu campfire gathering at a remote campground. As the flames danced in the darkness, fellow RVers shared stories of their adventures, creating a sense of camaraderie that transcended backgrounds and ages. The crackling fire became the backdrop to an evening filled with laughter, shared experiences, and newfound friendships.

3. Coastal Serenity in the Pacific Northwest:

Along the rugged coastline of the Pacific Northwest, waking up to the sound of crashing waves and the salty scent of the ocean became a daily ritual. Exploring secluded beaches, spotting whales in the distance, and witnessing breathtaking sunsets over the horizon made this leg of the journey a symphony of coastal serenity.

4. The Unexpected Wildlife Encounter:

A routine drive through a national park turned into a wildlife spectacle when a family of curious deer approached the RV. With awe-filled eyes, we watched as the deer grazed nearby, seemingly unbothered by our presence. It was a magical moment, a reminder of the untamed beauty that coexists with the nomadic lifestyle.

5. A Taste of Local Flavor:

Each destination brought a unique culinary adventure. From savoring beignets in the heart of New Orleans to indulging in fresh lobster on the shores of Maine, the RV journey became a gastronomic exploration of regional flavors. Every meal became a delightful chapter in the gastronomic diary of the road.

6. Full Moon Over the Desert Campsite:

Under the expansive desert sky, a full moon transformed the landscape into a surreal dreamscape. The quiet solitude of the desert night was punctuated only by the crackling campfire and the distant howls of coyotes. It was a celestial spectacle that etched a memory of profound stillness and natural beauty.

7. Mountain Majesty in the Rockies:

Navigating the winding roads of the Rocky Mountains revealed majestic vistas at every turn. Camping beneath snow-capped peaks, surrounded by alpine meadows and crystal-clear lakes, was a breathtaking experience. Hiking trails led to panoramic views, creating a sense of awe and reverence for the grandeur of the natural world.

8. Festival of Lights in a Coastal Town:

A chance visit to a charming coastal town coincided with a mesmerizing festival of lights. The RV park, adorned with colorful lanterns and illuminated displays, transformed into a magical wonderland. The laughter of children, the glow of lanterns, and the community spirit created a festive atmosphere that lingered in the memory.

These personal anecdotes from the road represent just a glimpse into the rich tapestry of RV experiences. Each story, whether born out of unexpected detours, chance encounters, or moments of quiet contemplation, contributes to the mosaic of memories that define the joy and adventure of life on the open road.

Conclusion

(Photo of RDNE Stock project httpswww.pexels.com)

In conclusion, the world of RV travel is a vast and exciting landscape, offering a unique blend of history, adventure, and community. This comprehensive guide, "Introduction to RV Travel," has been crafted to be a companion for both novice and seasoned RV enthusiasts, providing a roadmap to navigate the diverse and enriching experiences that come with life on the open road.

Engaging History:

The journey begins with a captivating exploration of the history of RVs. From their humble beginnings to becoming an iconic symbol of freedom and exploration in American travel culture, the evolution of RVs is a testament to the enduring spirit of adventure that drives enthusiasts to explore the vast landscapes of the United States.

Choosing the Right RV:

A crucial aspect of the RV lifestyle is choosing the right rig. The detailed analysis of buying versus renting offers readers a nuanced understanding of the financial and lifestyle considerations involved. Whether opting for ownership or the flexibility of renting, this guide equips readers to make informed decisions based on their unique preferences and circumstances.

Planning Your RV Adventure:

The section on route planning is a comprehensive guide to crafting the perfect RV journey. From utilizing tools and apps to consider scenic stops and points of interest, readers are empowered to design a route that aligns with their travel goals. The emphasis on itinerary flexibility encourages a spontaneous approach, allowing for serendipitous discoveries along the way.

RV Maintenance and Safety:

The importance of safety and proper maintenance is highlighted through a thorough pre-trip checklist and a beginner-friendly guide to basic RV maintenance. Ensuring the RV is in optimal condition before hitting the road is paramount, and this guide provides the essential know-how for a safe and enjoyable journey.

Navigating RV Parks and Campgrounds:

Choosing the right campgrounds is an art, and readers are educated on criteria such as amenities, location, and online reviews. Campground etiquette is also emphasized, fostering a sense of community and shared respect among fellow RVers.

Living Comfortably in Your RV:

The section on living comfortably delves into the essentials of packing and organization. From exhaustive packing lists to organizational hacks, readers are equipped with the tools to create a cozy and efficient living space within the confines of their RV.

Budgeting for RV Travel:

Financial considerations are demystified through a detailed breakdown of costs and practical money-saving tips. This section empowers readers to embark on their RV adventures with a clear understanding of the financial aspects involved.

Traveling with Family:

Families are not left out, with tailored suggestions for family-friendly activities and exploring education on the road. This ensures that RV travel becomes a fulfilling experience for all members of the family.

Working and RVing:

For those balancing work and travel, strategies for remote work and connectivity solutions are shared. This empowers RVers to maintain their professional lives while enjoying the freedom of the road.

Exploring National Parks and Landmarks:

The beauty of iconic national parks and landmarks is showcased, inviting readers to explore these breathtaking destinations. Suggestions for guided tours and activities enhance the exploration experience.

Culinary Adventures on the Road:

The culinary aspect of RV travel is not overlooked. RV cooking tips and regional cuisine exploration inspire readers to savor the diverse flavors encountered on their journeys.

Connecting with the RV Community:

The guide emphasizes the importance of community through socializing strategies and RV clubs. Building connections with fellow RV enthusiasts enriches the overall experience, turning the road into a communal adventure.

Environmental Responsibility:

Environmental consciousness is woven into the guide through Leave No Trace principles and eco-friendly practices. Encouraging responsible RVing fosters a culture of sustainability and preservation of the natural beauty that RV enthusiasts hold dear.

Overcoming Challenges:

The guide addresses potential challenges head-on, offering solutions for common issues and emphasizing the importance of emergency preparedness. Armed with knowledge and resources, readers can confidently tackle any hurdles they may encounter on their RV journeys.

Reflecting on the Journey:

The guide concludes with an invitation to reflect on the journey through journaling and documentation. Personal stories and anecdotes from the road serve as both inspiration and connection, reminding readers that the RV lifestyle is not just about the destinations but the stories and memories created along the way.

As readers embark on their RV adventures, may this guide serve as a trusted companion, offering insights, inspiration, and practical advice for a journey filled with discovery, camaraderie, and the boundless joy of the open road. Happy travels!

Made in the USA
Las Vegas, NV
05 September 2024

94810420R00059